The Protection Role and Jurisprudence of the United Nations Human Rights Council

Nijhoff Law Specials

VOLUME 106

The titles published in this series are listed at *brill.com/nlsp*

The Protection Role and Jurisprudence of the United Nations Human Rights Council

By

Bertrand Ramcharan

BRILL
NIJHOFF

LEIDEN | BOSTON

The Library of Congress Cataloging-in-Publication Data is available online at https://catalog.loc.gov

Typeface for the Latin, Greek, and Cyrillic scripts: "Brill". See and download: brill.com/brill-typeface.

ISSN 0924-4549
ISBN 978-90-04-50494-3 (paperback)
ISBN 978-90-04-50495-0 (e-book)

This book is printed on acid-free paper and produced in a sustainable manner.

Contents

Challenges of Protection

"Final Warning: Death Threats and Killings of Human Rights Defenders. Report of the Special Rapporteur on the Situation of Human Rights Defenders"
Submitted to the Human Rights Council at its 46th Session, Feb.-March, 2021[1]

"1 After having received death threats by phone for more than a year, environmental rights defender Fikile Ntshangase was shot dead in her home in Mtubatuba, South Africa, on the evening of 22 October, 2020 ...

"2 ... There is no more direct attack on civil society space than the killing of human rights defenders.

"3 ... In the period from 1 January 2019 to 30 June 2020 alone, the Special Rapporteur sent communications to 10 Member States on the killing of 100 human rights defenders, including 17 women human rights defenders.

"4 The Office of the United Nations High Commissioner for Human Rights (OHCHR) has observed that from 2015 to 2019, human rights defenders have been killed in at least 64 countries ... [listed] ... This represents nearly one third of Member States. ...

"9 The Special Rapporteur notes that many Governments are failing in their obligations to protect human rights defenders from attacks and killings by State and non-State actors. Some States, in particular those with high numbers of such killings, have established dedicated protection mechanisms to prevent and respond to risks and attacks against human rights defenders. While these mechanisms have been successful in part, human rights defenders often complain that the mechanisms are under- resourced, or that States lack the necessary political will to properly protect defenders. ...

"16 Human rights defenders working on some issues appear to be particularly vulnerable to attack. They include environmental human rights defenders, those protesting land grabs or those defending the rights of people, including indigenous peoples, by objecting to Governments that are imposing business projects on communities without free, prior and

1 A/HRC/46/35. Report dated 24 December, 2020 submitted by the Special Rapporteur Mary Lawlor to the 46th session of the UN Human Rights Council.

informed consent. One in two victims of killings recorded in 2019 by OHCHR had been working with communities around issues of land, environment, impacts of business activities, poverty and rights of indigenous peoples, Afro-descendants and other minorities. …

"33 The coming into force of the Regional Agreement on Access to Information, Public Participation and Justice in Environmental Matters in Latin America and the Caribbean (Escazu Agreement) is an important milestone. This is the first binding instrument that includes specific provisions for the protection and promotion of environmental human rights defenders …

"40 In 2019, OHCHR recorded the killing of 281 human rights defenders, including 38 women human rights defenders, and a total of 35 countries registered the killing of at least one human rights defender.

"41 Between 2015 and 2019, OHCHR recorded 1,323 killings of defenders, including 166 women and 22 young human rights defenders. …

"95 The Special Rapporteur is unable to respond to many of the reports she receives from defenders who have been targeted with death threats. A combination of a lack of resources in OHCHR dedicated to support the Special Rapporteur, and the length of the OHCHR process in responding to threats, means that it is not possible to react promptly under the mandate. This results in slow responses to information from defenders about threats they receive and sometimes no response at all, which is a matter of deep frustration to the Special Rapporteur. …

"106 OHCHR and other United Nations agencies should react faster to information on death threats to human rights defenders by increasing internal capacity at OHCHR dedicated to support the Special Rapporteur and by streamlining clearance procedures."

Philippines: UN Rights Office Appalled over Simultaneous Killings of 'Red-Tagged' Activists

UN News – 9 March, 2021 [while the Human Rights Council is in session]

Human Rights

The UN human rights office (OHCHR) said on Tuesday that it was 'appalled' by what appears to be the simultaneous arbitrary killings of nine activists in the Philippines during police-military operations in provinces surrounding the metropolitan area of the capital, Manila.

According to spokesperson Ravina Shamdasani, OHCHR received information stating that at around 3:15 am on Sunday, eight men and one woman were killed in Batangas, Cavite, Laguna and Rizal as police and military executed search warrants issued by a Manila court.

"We are deeply worried that these latest killings indicate an escalation in violence, intimidation, harassment and 'red-tagging' of human rights defenders', she said, noting a history of human rights advocates being 'red-tagged' – or accused of fronting for the armed wing of the Communist party."

Rights Activists in Crosshairs

Among those killed were labour rights activist Emanuel Asuncion, along with husband and wife Chai Lemita-Evangelista and Ariel Evangelista, who worked on issues relating to the rights of fishing communities and were reportedly shot inside their home. Melvin Dasigao and Mark Lee Coros were also among the victims, advocates for housing rights of people rendered homeless, according to OHCHR.

Two indigenous peoples' activists and two housing rights activists were also among those killed and six people were reportedly arrested during the operations.

"The Government has informed us that the operation was based on search warrants issued in the context of its counter-insurgency campaign against the New People's Army", Ms. Shamdasani said, briefing journalists in Geneva.

She pointed out that previous search warrants executed at night have also resulted in killings, including on 30 December when nine Tumandok indigenous peoples' rights activists were killed during joint operations, executing search warrants in Panay.

Strengthen Investigative Mechanisms

OHCHR welcomed the Government's commitment to investigate these cases, which it called "a critical test" for the domestic investigative mechanisms that it had established.

While the UN is working with the Government to strengthen these mechanisms, Ms Shamdasani stressed that they must be "prompt, transparent and effective" to meet international standards.

She detailed that the High Commissioner's June 2020 Human Rights Council report on the Philippines documented "a serious lack of due process in police operations, and near-total impunity for the use of lethal force by the police and the military".

In that report, the High Commissioner warned that "red-tagging" had proven extremely dangerous and urged the protection of human rights defenders, journalists and others at risk.

Call to Action

In recent months, there have been dozens of activists and several journalists arrested, including on Human Rights Day, 10 December.

"We urge the police to take urgent measures to prevent the use of excessive force resulting in loss of lives during law enforcement operations", the OHCHR spokesperson said.

"We also call on the Government and members of the security forces to refrain from rhetoric that may lead to violations, and instead make public commitments to uphold human rights and the rule of law."

The foregoing statement of the Office of the High Commissioner for Human Rights was issued while the Human Rights Council was in session. *There is no record of any action by the Council on this cry for help.*

Foreword

Adrien-Claude Zoller

Ever since the United Nations was established in 1945, victims, witnesses and civil society organisations have struggled to get it, and its principal human rights organ, now the *Human Rights Council*, to act for the protection of the human rights of victims of gross violations. This has been, and remains, an uphill struggle.

And yet, we must continue to strive for a stronger protection role for the United Nations and its Human Rights Council. Therein lies the importance of this new book of Professor Bertrand G. Ramcharan devoted to '*The protection role and jurisprudence of the UN Human Rights Council*'. It is a timely contribution by one of the best experts in the UN system to a necessary reflection on the achievements of the *Human Rights Council*, fifteen years after its creation by the UN General Assembly to replace the UN *Commission on Human Rights*.[2] The book carefully discusses how the *Human Rights Council*, with its strengths and weaknesses, has sought to provide a measure of protection. Implicit in the discussion is a quest to see how the Council can, in the future, expand and deepen its protection role.

It did not start in 2006. In his study, the author rightly refers to the main achievements of the United Nations, in particular with the *Commission on Human Rights* and its mechanisms. Step by step, in about forty years work and, sometimes hard, negotiations, the Commission and its Sub-Commission had elaborated General Principles of Law, Declarations, Conventions, treaty-monitoring bodies and Special procedures, all adopted by the Economic and Social Council (ECOSOC) and the General Assembly. In its *Vienna Declaration and Programme of Action* (VDPA), the 1993 World Conference on Human Rights (WCHR),[3] had confirmed this emerging world human rights system. The WCHR had also paved the way to the creation of the post of the *High Commissioner for Human Rights*, which would strongly change the role of the Secretariat of the United Nations.

The Vienna consensus was soon tested in the new challenges the UN faced in the 90s. Firstly, the end of the Cold War led to many local and regional

2 General Assembly resolution 60/251 of 15 March 2006.

3 WCHR, held in Vienna from 14 to 25 June 1993.

conflicts. Peace and security had to be assured by the UN. In a few years, the *UN Security Council* had to increase the number of its peace-keeping operations. In severe situations, it had to create *Commissions of inquiries* and even *Special Tribunals* for war crimes and crimes against humanity (former-Yugoslavia, Rwanda, Cambodia, Sierra Leone, Timor, Lebanon).

Secondly, after the Cold War there was *one economic system* only. One could not continue to ignore the existing link between economics and human rights, especially with the rapid globalization process. Widespread extreme poverty and the gaps in income distribution, both inside and between the countries, dramatically increased. Largely neglected during the Cold War, the demands of the countries from the South then resurfaced.

Finally, as the system was expanding exponentially with new tasks, programmes, entities, the United Nations was facing major challenges in decision-making, management and finance. It needed in-depth reorganisation.

It is in this context that the new UN Secretary General Kofi Annan had launched, in January 1997, an ambitious *Reform of the UN*.[4] Together with the outcomes of several UN world conferences in the 90s (on development and environment, human rights, habitat, population, women), the Reform process led to major changes, including in the human rights machinery. Under the impulsion of Annan, High Level Groups of experts had been set-up. The Assembly endorsed most of the recommendations contained in his successive reports, such as the reorganisation of the UN Secretariat into four sectors (security; economic and social affairs; humanitarian affairs; development); the merger of UN Geneva-based human rights entities into one single *Office of the High Commissioner for Human Rights* (OHCHR), led by the High Commissioner; the creations of a *Senior Management Group* (including with the High Commissioner for Human Rights); and of the post of Deputy Secretary-General; and, later, the strengthening of the *national protection systems* through the country teams and country coordinators, and the creation of UN Women.

This process had been boosted by the *Millennium Summit*.[5] Its landmark *United Nations Millennium Declaration* reaffirmed the commitment to the Charter's purposes and principles, including '*to respect fully and uphold the Universal Declaration*'; to strive for the full protection and promotion in all their countries of all the rights for all; and to achieve by the year 2015 the '*Millennium Development Goals*' (MDGS).

4 See in particular the Report of the Secretary-General, '*Renewing the United Nations: A Programme for Reform*' (A/51/950), 14 July 1997.

5 Millennium Summit, held in New York from 6 to 8 September 2000.

Following the Millennium Summit, a High Level Panel on '*Threats, Challenges & Change*' was constituted under the Chairmanship of former Prime Minister Anand Panyarachun (Thailand). In its Report of 2 December 2004 entitled '*A more secure world: our shared responsibility*',[6] the Panel reaffirmed the UN human rights commitment. However, it strongly criticized the way the Commission was functioning, blaming in particular member States, and concluding: '*Member States should consider upgrading the Commission to become a 'Human Rights Council' that is no longer subsidiary to the Economic and Social Council but a Charter body standing alongside it and the Security Council*'.[7]

Annan endorsed the views of the Panel in his famous report '*In Larger Freedom*', submitting proposals for the September 2005 World Summit.[8] He supported the creation of a Human Rights Council with a '*peer review*' of the situation in all the members States, and affirmed: '*Yet the Commission's capacity to perform its tasks has been increasingly undermined by its declining credibility and professionalism. In particular, States have sought membership of the Commission not to strengthen human rights but to protect themselves against criticism or to criticize others. As a result, a credibility deficit has developed, which casts a shadow on the reputation of the United Nations system as a whole (…) If the United Nations is to meet the expectations of men and women everywhere – and indeed, if the Organization is to take the cause of human rights as seriously as those of security and development – then Member States should agree to replace the Commission on Human Rights with a smaller standing Human Rights Council*'[9].

Less than twenty years after these statements and after the 2005 Summit of Heads of States and Government, which endorsed this proposal, one may have difficulty to understand the reasons for such criticism of the Commission and its Sub-Commission. In fact, it mainly concerned the way the two bodies dealt

6 '*A more secure world: our shared responsibility*'. Document A/59/565. The Panel was chaired by Anand Panyarachun, former Prime Minister of Thailand, the Panel was composed of Robert Badinter (France), Joâo Baena Soares (Brazil), Gro Harlem Brundtland (Norway), Mary Chinery Hesse (Ghana), Gareth Evans (Australia), David Hannay (United Kingdom of Great Britain and Northern Ireland), Enrique Iglesias (Uruguay), Amre Moussa (Egypt), Satish Nambiar (India), Sadako Ogata (Japan), Yevgeny Primakov (Russian Federation), Qian Qiqian (China), Salim Salim (United Republic of Tanzania), Nafis Sadik (Pakistan) and Brent Scowcroft (United States of America).

7 '*A more secure world: our shared responsibility*', paragraph 291.

8 'In larger freedom: towards development, security and human rights for all' (A/59/2005), Report of the Secretary-General, 21 March 2005.

9 'In larger freedom, paragraphs 182–183.

with situations of massive human rights abuses. On the one hand, though targeted States invoked States sovereignty and non interference to oppose scrutiny, they could not prevent a growing number of country resolutions and mechanisms to be adopted. These (authoritarian) regimes then increased pressure on the Sub-Commission, whose experts at a certain moment even requested (and obtained) the right to vote country resolutions by secret ballot. Gradually, in the 90s, the power of the Sub-Commission to adopt country resolutions was reduced. The Commission ultimately stated that the experts could discuss country situations, but that they '*should not adopt country-specific resolutions* (...) and refrain from '*adopting thematic resolutions containing references to specific countries*'.[10] Attacks also increased in the 90s against members of the Sub-Commission and even Special Rapporteurs of the Commission. Pressure and even reprisals affected human rights NGOs cooperating with the Commission and its mechanisms. In the 90s, many States elaborated policies to control victims, witnesses and civil society organisations, and to prevent them to submit their information to the mechanisms of the United Nations.

On the other hand, defenders deplored that the Commission did not act on serious cases of violations. Year after year the European Union resolution on the situation in China was defeated, as each time the Chinese Delegation successfully tabled *no-action motions*. A '*Like-Minded Group*' (LMG) emerged, denouncing this '*politicization*', this '*partiality*', and opposing any country resolutions. Many hardliner States sought and obtained membership of the Commission to protect themselves. As a result, at the end of the 90s, most of the States, those advocating the end of country resolutions, and those deploring the lack of action on China and other hardliner States, spoke of the '*discredited Commission*'.

Fifteen years after the replacement of the Commission by the Council, it is therefore time to assess the Human Rights Council whether and how far the Council made a difference and achieved progress in the field of protection.

Herein lies the importance of this book. Obviously, on a scale of one to ten, it would be hard to assess United Nations protection at more than five. The simple fact of the matter is that there are still numerous groups suffering gross violations, or at risk of such violations, who receive little or no protection from the United Nations.

The protection of human rights is preventive protection, reactive protection, and remedial protection. To put it simply, inside the Human Rights Council there is a small measure of preventive protection. There is a fair measure of

10 Commission on Human Rights, Decision 2000/109, 56th session.

reactive protection, but this is very uneven and often subject to political calculations. And there is a tiny amount of remedial protection.

After reading this thoughtful and well documented book the reader will, hopefully, be stimulated to consider how the protection role of the Human Rights Council can be made stronger in the future.

One of the merits of the book is its discussion, for the first time ever in the literature, of the 'jurisprudence' of the Human Rights Council. The idea behind this discussion is to trace how the Human Rights Council, with its strengths and weaknesses, contributes to the future normative architecture of protection in life and death areas facing humanity, such as climate change.

The Human Rights Council, notwithstanding the politicization that characterises its deliberations and decisions, nevertheless reflects the aspirations of humankind for a fairer and more just world. This normative/jurisprudential contribution of the Council is among its worthwhile contributions to international law and relations.

It is now fifty years since Professor Bertrand Ramcharan, an active Board Member of *Geneva for Human Rights*, entered the service of the United Nations, where he rose to perform the functions of UN High Commissioner for Human Rights as Under-Secretary-General. He has been an architect of UN human rights strategy for half a century – something I have been fortunate to witness first-hand. The enhancement of the protection role of the United Nations has been a consistent theme running through his work and writings. He continues this quest in the present work, a worthwhile contribution to reflections on the role and future of the Human Rights Council.

I commend this important book to the attention of the human rights community.

Adrien-Claude Zoller
President
Geneva for Human Rights
6 January 2022

Preface

Antony Blinken, US Secretary of State and a long-time human rights champion, summarised the UN Human Rights Council aptly at the start of the Biden Administration in the USA: "When it works well, the Human Rights Council shines a spotlight on countries with the worst human rights records and can serve as an important forum for those fighting injustice and tyranny."[11] At the same time, Blinken recognized "that the Human Rights Council is a flawed body, in need of reform to its agenda, membership and focus, including its disproportionate focus on Israel"[12] but he thought that "positive change" could be made within the Council.

Yes, the Human Rights Council has its merits and its flaws. Blinken thought, for example, that "the Council could help to promote the fundamental rights of women, girls, LGBTQI+ persons and other marginalized communities."[13] At the same time, the Financial times pointed out that the body "includes Russia, Venezuela and China, which the US has accused of committing genocide against Uighur Muslims in Xinjiang province. Eritrea, Mauritania and Pakistan are other members regularly cited for violations."[14]

Human rights NGOs continue to invest much efforts and hopes that the Human Rights Council can be coaxed into acting for the prevention, mitigation, and remedy of gross violations of human rights and to foster human rights justice in the world. Thus, on 17 February, 2021, on the eve of

11 "US returns to UN human rights body", Financial Times, London, 9 February, 2021, p.4. On 10 October, 2021, upon the election of the USA to membership of the Council, Secretary-of-State Blinken issued a statement in which he offered the following assessment of the Human Rights Council: "The Council plays a meaningful role in protecting human rights and fundamental freedoms by documenting atrocities in order to hold wrongdoers accountable. It focuses attention on emergencies and unfolding human rights crises, ensuring that those who are voiceless have a place to be heard. The Council provides a forum where we can have open discussions about ways we and our partners can improve. At the same time, it also suffers from serious flaws, including disproportionate attention on Israel and the membership of several states with egregious human rights records. Together, we must push back against attempts to subvert the ideals upon which the Human Rights Council was founded, including that each person is endowed with human rights and that states are obliged to protect those tights." – Press Release by the US Department of State, 14 October, 2021.

12 Ibid.

13 Ibid.

14 Ibid.

the 46th session of the Council, the International Service for Human Rights issued a release in which it stated the following:

> The 46th session of the UN Human Rights Council, from 22 February to 23 March, will consider issues including the protection of human rights defenders, systemic racism, police brutality and violence against peaceful protests – particularly in the United States of America, freedom of religion or belief, protection and promotion of human rights while countering terrorism, human rights situations in States including Nicaragua, Venezuela, Occupied Palestinian Territory including East Jerusalem, Syria, South Sudan, Sri Lanka, Burundi, Iran, the Democratic People's Republic of Korea, Myanmar, Eritrea, among many others.[15]

The human rights community will probably be heartened by some actions of the Council on these issues and situations, and will undoubtedly be disappointed by the Council's failure to act on others. Nevertheless, Governments, NGOs and special procedures of the Council will have had opportunities to air their concerns before the Council and that would probably give a measure of solace to the victims of gross violations.

The Human Rights Council is a political body mandated to act on the basis of human rights principles. Principle and politics coexist uneasily within the Council, with politics trumping principle on many occasions. The Council should stand for the universality of human rights; it should act for the promotion and protection of human rights, the prevention of human rights violations, the protection of victims of violations and for justice for the victims of such violations. At the same time, its founding resolution encourages it to act through cooperation and dialogue, which numerous members of the Council interpret as meaning that the Council should not condemn countries, even when they are committing egregious violations of human rights. This is hard to swallow for believers in the universal protection of human rights, including this author.

Against this background it might, at first sight, seem strange to write a book on The Protection Role and Jurisprudence of the UN Human Rights Council. We think, however, that this could still be a worthwhile effort. The Human Rights Council is the principal UN body specifically tasked with the promotion and protection of human rights and it could be useful to gather up the positive

---

15 International Service for Human Rights, "HRC 46/ Key Issues on agenda of March 2021 session, 17 February, 2021, p. 1.

elements of its practice as building blocks for the future protection of human rights at the United Nations. This is particularly important at a time of growing great power contestation in the world over values, principles, and strategies.

At the end of the day, it is the United Nations, for all of its challenges, that helps define universal values and principles of protection, through the International Court of Justice, human rights treaty bodies, the Security Council, the General Assembly, and its subsidiary organ, the Human Rights Council. The United Nations is the leading arbiter of what is universal.

It has long been established that political organs of the United Nations can contribute to the progressive development of international law.[16] In this book we shall endeavour to identify such contributions by the Human Rights Council when it comes to its protection role and jurisprudence.

The method we shall follow in discussing the ten thematic chapters in this book will be to present, in a flexible manner: the mandate of the Council, the relevant normative or policy framework, selected evidence from the practice of the Council, comments on that practice, some recommendations, and a synthesis of our findings at the end.

16 See, e.g. Rosalyn Higgins, The Development of International Law Through the Political Organs of the United Nations, London, Royal Institute of International Affairs, 1963.

Introduction

The story of human rights at the UN is one of constant struggle and striving to overcome political obstacles to the protection of victims of gross violations. When the UN Charter was being drafted, the great powers objected to including in the mandate of the UN a competence to protect human rights. Instead, the Charter refers to promotion and to international cooperation for the universal realization of human rights.[1] It would take considerable effort to develop an incipient protection capacity in the world body. Part of this story is told in The Advent of Universal Protection of Human Rights: Theo van Boven and the Transformation of the UN Role.[2]

In 1947, the then Commission on Human Rights adopted an infamous resolution that it lacked competence to consider the thousands of petitions reaching it from victims of gross violations of human rights, including victims in Eastern Europe and Afro-Americans in the USA. The then UN Assistant Secretary-General in charge of human rights, Henri Laugier, denounced this decision as shameful. It would take consistent lobbying from NGOs over nearly twenty-five years to get a resolution from the Economic and Social Council authorising the Commission on Human Rights to identify and take limited action on situations that appeared to reveal a consistent pattern of reliably attested gross violations of human rights.[3]

Between 1970 and 2005, when the Commission was replaced by the Human Rights Council, some eighty-four country situations had been discussed in the Commission, exchanges carried out with government representatives, and some missions undertaken to countries for discreet discussions with governments in an effort to generate protection of victims. On paper, this procedure still exists within the Human Rights Council but it has been overcast by a reluctance on the part of some Members of the Council to engage in 'confrontational approaches' towards governments accused of committing gross violations of human rights.

In 1965, the newly independent countries entering the United Nations in large numbers moved a resolution in the UN General Assembly calling upon the Commission on Human Rights to act on allegations of gross violations of human rights in any part of the world, particularly in colonial and in dependent

1 This story is told, with the accompanying documents, in L.Sohn and T. Buergenthal, The International Protection of Human Rights. Indiana, Bobbs Merril, 1973.

2 Springer, Cham, Switzerland, 2019. (Bertrand Ramcharan, author).

3 ECOSOC resolution 1503 (XLVIII).

 | DOI:10.1163/9789004504950_002

territories. The result was that, from 1967 onwards, the Commission engaged in public debate about allegations of gross violations of human rights. Grievances were aired, telegrams sent to Governments, resolutions adopted expressing concern or condemning governments responsible, and a few fact-finding missions were established. The Commission established a system of country and thematic fact-finders, known as special procedures, and they played an important role in exposing gross violations of human rights.[4]

The successor to the Commission, the present-day Human Rights Council, inherited these special procedures but, from the outset, began to press them for more dialogue and cooperation and less 'confrontational' approaches. This has placed a dampener on the open consideration of allegations of gross violations of human rights. An effort was even made to adopt a draconian code of conduct for special procedures mandate holders but, fortunately, this did not go through as initially planned, even if a code of conduct was still adopted.

Alongside the foregoing approaches built on the foundations of the UN Charter, a strong jurisprudence of protection has been developed within petitions procedures established under human rights treaties, such as the Optional Protocol to the International Covenant on Civil and Political Rights.[5] Unfortunately, human rights treaty bodies are also under increasing pressure from governments to engage in more cooperation and dialogue and less 'confrontation'.

The establishment of the International Criminal Court was intended to strengthen international protection of human rights and it may yet fulfil this aspiration in time. However, the Court has come under pressure from major powers, such as the USA, which vehemently objects to the Court's prosecutor investigating allegations against American soldiers in places such as Afghanistan and Iraq, and from some African countries that think the Court has had too much of a focus on Africa. The USA, during the Trump administration, even prohibited the then prosecutor from entering the USA and froze her assets in that country, a vile act indeed.

In its founding resolution, the Human Rights Council has a clear mandate to act for the universal promotion and protection of human rights and for the prevention of human rights violations.[6] At the same time, the resolution establishing the Council encourages it to pursue cooperation and dialogue,

4 See on this, B.G. Ramcharan, The Concept and Present Status of the International Protection of Human Rights. The Hague, Martinus Nijhoff, 1988.

5 See, e.g., J. Th Moller and A. de Zayas, The Case Law of the UN Human Rights Committee under the Optional Protocol. Kiel, Engel Publishers, 2009.

6 See General Assembly resolution 60/251 of 15 March, 2006, which established the Council.

which the majority of its membership has so far interpreted as giving priority to approaches of dialogue and cooperation over principled pronouncements against gross violations of human rights. In truth, cooperation and dialogue should be carried out with a view to the principled protection of human rights[7] and not in opposition to such principled action.

Notwithstanding these vexing political attitudes, the Human Rights Council has been able to develop an incipient protection role and to put down some building blocks in a jurisprudence of protection. The human rights fact-finders of the Council, collectively known as its Special Procedures, continue to undertake urgent action to help protect victims, visit countries, issue appeals, and submit reports documenting gross violations. The Council has so far met in some thirty special sessions convened to discuss urgent human rights situations. Occasionally, but admittedly selectively, the Council has adopted resolutions roundly condemning gross violations of human rights. It has admittedly overlooked many situations where such condemnation would be warranted.

In these circumstances it may be constructive to view human rights efforts within the United Nations as one of incremental progress and, step by step, to strive to assemble further building blocks of protection. The UN Charter and the Universal Declaration represent a core commitment to uphold human rights universally. Around this core principle, which we may term the centre of commitment, there is a small circle of achievement represented by the norms and jurisprudence so far developed and by efforts to encourage the strengthening of national protection systems.

Outside of this inner circle of achievement, there is another circle that one might term the circle of opportunities for further progress. At the time of writing, for example, it would be of some importance to advance the protection of human rights in the face of climate change. Beyond the first two circles, there is a much wider circle containing all the problems confronting humanity to achieve universal realization of economic and social rights, civil and political rights, and to render justice to the victims of gross violations.

This book is influenced by this incremental – and hopefully optimistic – perspective. We begin, in chapter one, by briefly noting the promotional activities of the Council that contribute to protection. In Chapter two we look at the United Nations philosophy of the universality of human rights that should inspire and guide the Council. In chapter three we consider principles of protection that should guide the Council. In chapter four we discuss the Council's

7 See on this, Bertrand Ramcharan, Contemporary Human Rights Ideas. London, Routledge, Second edition, 2015.

efforts, in fits and starts so far, to pursue the prevention of gross violations. In chapter five we look at efforts of urgent action and mitigation of gross violations. In chapter six we try to identify instances of the exercise of good offices on behalf of victims of violations, while in chapter seven we present the fact-finding experience of the Council. In Chapter eight we discuss whether the Council has been able to pursue redress for gross violations in some instances. In chapter nine we discuss what role the principle of justice plays in the Council. We try to see whether, over some fifty sessions and some thirty special sessions to date, one might be able to distil some principles of justice from its practice. A final chapter, ten, discusses the jurisprudence of the Council, after which we try to draw these different strands together in some concluding observations.

The method we shall follow in discussing the ten thematic chapters in this book will be to present, in a flexible manner: the mandate of the Council, the relevant normative or policy framework, selected evidence from the practice of the Council, comments on that practice, some recommendations, and a synthesis of our findings at the end.

CHAPTER 1

Promoting Protection

1 Introduction

There is an extraordinary amount of good promotional work done by the Human Rights Council or by its subsidiary bodies that contributes to the protection of human rights in the long-term and in many instances in the near-term. This being a book about the protection role of the Council, we shall, in this chapter, provide a concise overview of the Council's promotional work that contributes to protection.

2 The Universal Periodic Review

At intervals of four and a half years, every Member of the United Nations submits a report to the Council on its efforts to uphold human rights. Alongside the report of the Government are reports submitted by the Office of the UN High Commissioner for Human Rights (OHCHR) on the findings and observations of human rights treaty bodies and by human rights fact-finders of the Council. The submitting Government responds to questions from fellow States and to a lesser extent from NGOs and national human rights institutions.

The process has its strengths and its flaws. A Government participating in good faith, wishing to partake of the experiences of its peers, can learn about new ways of advancing the cause of human rights in its country. On the other hand, a government participating perfunctorily or in bad faith can attempt to pull wool over the eyes of its peers.

The ultimate rationale of the process is to help Governments strengthen, or establish, when they do not yet exist, adequate and effective national protection systems. It has great promise if cooperation takes place in good faith.

3 Standard-Setting

The Human Rights Council has continued the practice of its predecessor, the Commission on Human Rights, of facilitating the preparation and adoption of new standards in areas where they are needed for the protection of human rights against new risks. Standards for the protection of the environment and

 | DOI:10.1163/9789004504950_003

to combat climate change are two examples of areas where standard-setting activities within the Council are underway.[1]

4 Cooperation with National Human Rights Institutions

National Human Rights Institutions established in some countries, which are in compliance with international standards for such institutions (The Paris Principles), participate actively in the meetings and other procedures of the Human Rights Council, including the UPR. At the end of the day, human rights need to be promoted and protected inside each country. National human rights institutions can play an important part in this process. International cooperation for human rights should aim at the emplacement, in all countries, of adequate and effective independent national protection systems that are adequately resourced with constitutional, legislative, judicial, institutional, protective, preventive and educational dimensions

5 Business and Human Rights

The Human Rights Council has adopted standards calling on businesses to play their part in the promotion and protection of human rights. It has a Working Group on Business and Human Rights that does good work on this topic. The Working Group on Business and Human Rights chairs and guides a regular UN Forum on business and human rights. The drafting of standards on Business and human rights started under the predecessor of the Council, the Commission on Human Rights. Under the Council, work in this area has gained in amplitude and intensity.

6 Indigenous Populations

Continuing the work of its predecessor, the Human Rights Council took forward the drafting of what was eventually adopted by the General Assembly as the Declaration on the rights of Indigenous Peoples. Under its predecessor, the Commission on Human Rights, there was a Working Group of its Sub-Commission devoted to this topic, as well as a Special Rapporteur. Now the

1 See on this, Chapter 10 below, Jurisprudence.

Human Rights Council has a Special Rapporteur and an Expert mechanism on the rights of indigenous peoples. These specialised mechanisms gather information on the situation of indigenous peoples world-wide, interact and dialogue with indigenous representatives, visit countries with indigenous peoples, engage in urgent appeals on their behalf when necessary, and engage in various other activities intended to promote and protect the rights of indigenous peoples.

7 Minorities

The former Commission on Human Rights undertook various activities to promote and protect the rights of minorities. The Human Rights Council has taken forward these activities and strives to promote and protect the rights of minorities. It has an Independent Expert on Minority Issues who reports to the Council regularly and holds annually a Forum on Minority Issues.

8 Slavery and Slavery-Like Practices

Unfortunately, slavery and slavery-like practices continue in several parts of the world. The former Commission on Human Rights had an expert group on this problem. The Human Rights Council has taken forward these activities, and there is now a Special Rapporteur on slavery who monitors manifestations of slavery and slavery-like practices on a world-wide basis and acts for their elimination and prevention, and for the protection of victims.

9 Racism and Racial Discrimination

The Council has been energetic in its efforts to combat racism and racial discrimination. A good example of this is resolution 48/14 adopted on 11 October, 2021[2] focussing on "From rhetoric to reality: a global call for concrete action against racism, racial discrimination, xenophobia and related intolerance". In this resolution, the Council underscored the importance of political will and commitment to eliminate all forms of racism, racial discrimination, xenophobia and related intolerance.

2 Adopted on a recorded vote of 32 to 10, with 5 abstentions.

The Council expressed its continuing alarm at the resurgent violent manifestations of racism, racial discrimination, xenophobia and related intolerance precipitated by scientifically false, morally condemnable, socially unjust and dangerous ideologies, such as white supremacy, as well as by extremist nationalist and populist ideologies, and underlined in this respect that human beings are born free and equal in dignity and rights and that everyone has the right to life, liberty and security of persons.

The Council has a number of subsidiary bodies engaged on these and related issues, including: (1) An *Ad Hoc* Committee on the Elaboration of Complementary Standards to the International Convention on the Elimination of All Forms of Racial Discrimination. (2) An Intergovernmental Working Group on the Effective Implementation of the Durban Declaration and Programme of Action. (3) A Group of Independent Eminent Experts on the Implementation of the Durban Declaration and Programme of Action. (4) Its Advisory Committee, which it mandated to prepare a study examining patterns, policies and processes contributing to incidents of racial discrimination. (5) An International Decade for People of African Descent. (6) A Permanent Forum on People of African Descent.

10 Human Rights Defenders

The Council has regularly condemned all acts of intimidation or reprisal, both online and offline, by State and non-State actors against individuals and groups who seek to cooperate, cooperate or have cooperated with the United Nations, its representatives and mechanisms in the field of human rights. In a resolution adopted without a vote on 8 October, 2021, the Council urged all States to prevent and refrain from all acts of intimidation or reprisal, both online and offline, against those who:

(a) Seek to cooperate, cooperate or have cooperated with the United Nations, its representatives and mechanisms in the field of human rights, or who have provided testimony or information to them;

(b) Avail or have availed themselves of procedures established under the auspices of the United Nations for the protection of human rights and fundamental freedoms, and all those who have provided legal or other assistance to them for this purpose;

(c) Submit or have submitted communications under procedures established by human rights instruments, and all those who have provided legal or other assistance to them for this purpose;

(d) Are relatives of victims of human rights violations or those who have provided legal or other assistance to victims.

The Council encouraged the UN Assistant Secretary-General for Human Rights to strengthen efforts to develop and implement at the United Nations level a more comprehensive system for preventing and addressing allegations of acts of intimidation or reprisal, including by information-gathering and data analysis, and by improving and coordinating the response by all United Nations actors, and, in this regard, called upon all States and relevant stakeholders to contribute to these efforts.

The Council welcomed the steps taken by the President of the Council on these issues and encouraged the President to continue, in consultation with the States concerned, to use her or his good offices to address as appropriate allegations of acts of intimidation or reprisal against those who seek to cooperate, cooperate or have cooperated with the Council, and to provide information on cases brought to her or his attention at each session of the Council.[3]

11 Studies

As evolving human rights problems surface in the world, the Human Rights Council turns to its Advisory Committee, a group of experts, to prepare studies and make recommendations on them. To date, the Advisory Committee has done studies on a variety of topics, including the following, listed chronologically, starting with the most recent:

- Racial equality
- Negative effects of terrorism
- Representation of women in human rights organizations and mechanisms
- New and emerging digital technologies
- National policies and human rights.
- A legally-binding instrument on the right to development
- Technical assistance and capacity building for human rights
- Illicit funds
- Regional arrangements for the promotion and protection of human rights
- The activities of vulture funds
- Leprosy-related discrimination
- Unaccompanied migrant children and adolescents

---

3 Resolution 48/17, Cooperation with the United Nations, its representatives and mechanisms in the field of human rights.

- Human rights in post-disaster and conflict situations
- Negative impact of corruption
- Human rights and unilateral coercive measures
- Attacks on persons with albinism
- Promoting human rights through sport and the Olympic ideal
- Local government and human rights
- Promoting human rights and fundamental freedoms through a better understanding of traditional values of human-kind
- Human rights and issues related to hostage-taking
- Human rights and international solidarity
- Enhancement of international cooperation in the field of human rights
- Right to peace
- Missing persons
- Right to food
- Human rights education and training.[4]

12 Human Rights Education and Training

Based on the work of its Advisory Committee, the Human Rights Council endorsed and referred to the General Assembly for adoption, a draft Declaration on Human Rights Education and Training. The aim was to encourage education and training on human rights within all countries. The General Assembly adopted the declaration and called upon governments to implement its provisions.

13 Country Rapporteurs, Thematic Rapporteurs and Working Groups

Under a system usually referred to as the 'Special Procedures', the Human Rights Council has some fifty country rapporteurs, thematic rapporteurs, and working groups who study, gather information, engage in urgent action, visit countries, make recommendations, and sometimes put forward drafts of new standards for consideration by the Council. This is a combination of promotional and protection work.

4 Source: Office of the High Commissioner for Human Rights.

14 World Campaign on Human Rights

The Human Rights Council has taken forward the work of its predecessor in running world campaigns on human rights meant to spread and entrench worldwide a universal culture of human rights. In a resolution on combatting racism and racial discrimination that it adopted at its forty-eighth session, the Council requested the United Nations system to strengthen its awareness-raising campaigns to increase the visibility of the message of the Durban Declaration and programme of Action, its follow-up mechanisms and the work of the United Nations in the fight against racism. It requested the Secretariat to carry out an outreach and a public information campaign for the commemoration of the twentieth anniversary of the Durban Declaration and Programme of Action. Furthermore, it requested the Office of High Commissioner for Human Rights to establish and launch a two-year comprehensive communications strategy, inclusive of an outreach programme to raise awareness about and mobilize global public support for racial equality.[5]

15 Cooperation with Related UN Organs

The Human Rights Council regularly cooperates with other United Nations organs, such as the UN Peacebuilding Commission, in an effort to advance the integration of human rights into United Nations peace operations.

16 Cooperation with Regional Human Rights Bodies

The Human Rights Council also has cooperative relations with regional human rights bodies such as the Council of Europe, the African Commission on Human and Peoples Rights, the Inter-American Commission on Human Rights, and the ASEAN Commission on Human Rights.

17 Conclusion

The volume of work undertaken within, and under the auspices of the Human Rights Council is massive. Much of it is valuable promotional, educational and

5 Resolution 48/18, adopted on a recorded vote of 32 to 10, with 5 abstentions.

disseminating work. Its aim is to entrench, world-wide, a universal culture of human rights. The aim of promotion is to facilitate protection. Promotional work is intended to protect human rights, now and in the future.

Public comments on the Human Rights Council tend to focus on political controversies and overlook the Council's valuable promotional work. There is also a lot of special pleading by Governments accused of gross violations of human rights. It is part of their strategy to denigrate the Council and the overall human rights framework.

Nevertheless, it is right that the principal human rights body of the UN be held to a high standard when it comes to the protection of human rights. This is the reason that our focus, in the rest of this book, will be on the protection role and jurisprudence of the Council.

CHAPTER 2

Universality

1 Introduction

The UN General Assembly resolution establishing the Human Rights Council commits it to upholding the universality of human rights, as well as the indivisibility and interdependence of civil and political rights and economic, social and cultural rights. Under the Universal Periodic Review process that the Council has run since its establishment, every Government has participated by submitting a report, now at intervals of four and a half years. Every Government has formally subscribed to the universality of human rights. The peer review process operates on the assumption of universality. One could therefore say that, at the formal level, the Human Rights Council subscribes to the universality of human rights.

The Vienna Declaration of Human Rights (1993) and the UN Millennium Declaration (2000) both have ringing affirmations of the universality of human rights. Paragraph 1 of the Vienna Declaration held forth that "The universal nature of these rights and freedoms is beyond question". Paragraph 25 of the Millennium Declaration stated: "We resolve … to respect fully and uphold the Universal Declaration of Human Rights; to strive for the full protection and promotion in all our countries of civil, political, economic, social and cultural rights for al."

It is good that, at the formal level, the Human Rights Council continues to profess adherence to the universality of human rights. It even says so in resolutions adopted from time to time. But just beneath the surface there are potentially volcanic rumblings putting universality under challenge. In the Council itself it has, since its establishment applied different weights and measures to different situations. Universality of protection is distinctly lacking in the Council. Then, there are powerful overt and covert challenges to universality at the United Nations, including inside the Human Rights Council. Under the Trump Administration, the US State Department established a Commission, chaired by a leading Harvard University Law Professor, that sought to re-define the concept of inalienable rights with a view to reducing the number of such rights. The Chinese Government openly seeks to re-define the content of international law and to challenge the notion of universality. The Russian Government is an advocate of sovereign rights over individual rights. India, formerly the largest democracy in the world with a tradition of the rule of law,

 DOI:10.1163/9789004504950_004

openly flouts international norms of human rights. Saudi Arabia, the custodian of the two most holy places of Islam, asserts the primacy of Islamic Law, as do other countries. Influential countries such as Turkey and Egypt openly flout international norms of human rights.

In short, inside the Human Rights Council, the focus of attention in this book, a light web of universality is holding back, for the time being, potentially volcanic eruptions that can sweep universality away. It is important to start the journey of this book by recognizing the constant danger of a volcanic eruption. In the course of this chapter, we shall look briefly at the Universal Periodic Review process; discuss the universality of human rights philosophically and under international law; note some of the global challenges to universality; and make the case for the universality of human rights world-wide. It is our view that if the United Nations and its Human Rights Council fail to uphold the universality of human rights, the struggle for human rights will have changed dramatically for the worse.

2 The Universal Periodic Review

The Universal Periodic Review process is a promotional one that can help countries steer a course towards stronger national protection systems – if they wish to pursue such a course. It is potentially useful. If well-meaning governments approach the process in good faith, involve civil society in the preparation of their reports, cooperate in good faith in listening to the views of their peers, take follow-up actions in good faith, again in consultation with civil society, then the process can yield positive results inside the country.

Unfortunately, many, perhaps most, of the Governments submitting reports are undemocratic or corrupt ones that write glossy reports far removed from the realities in their countries, and often with little or no consultation with civil society. In the Human Rights Council, they lobby their bedfellows to praise them or to ask soft questions. They are at liberty to accept or not to accept recommendations made by their peers. NGOs are not allowed to speak at the stage when the Government's report is discussed, but are given limited opportunities to speak when the report of the Working Group of the whole is discussed in the plenary Human Rights Council.

The report of the Working Group of the whole records the proceedings, the comments, and the recommendations, which can be quite voluminous. After the report is discussed in the plenary, the Human Rights Council simply notes the report. It does not express a view on the situation of human rights in the country or on the content of the report before it. Many countries reliably accused of grossly violating human rights pass through the UPR process without reprimand.

In the cycles of the UPR process after the first, the Human Rights Council focuses on the implementation of recommendations made in the earlier cycles. The submitting Government remains in the driver's seat, whatever its record on human rights. Again, there is no deep scrutiny of the human rights record of the country. One thing is clear: the UPR process is not a barometer of human rights universality in practice. It may have universalist objectives, and in the very, very, long term, it might contribute to the universal spread of human rights on the ground. But, for the time being, it is often an Alice in wonderland process.

In real life, a dangerous struggle is under way, as major powers overtly and covertly challenge universality, as we shall see later in this chapter. We first set out, next the philosophical bases of universality and thereafter the status of universality in international law.

3 Philosophical Universality

The thesis of universal values is supported by leading philosophers, such as Immanuel Kant, Rabindranath Tagore, and Isiah Berlin. Berlin thought that there was 'value pluralism' in the world, but this did not preclude the existence of core universal values. A recent issue of *Philosophy*, the Journal of the Royal Institute of Philosophy in the United Kingdom, carried an editorial on the contemporary significance of human rights, asserting in the process, that its roots lay in Enlightenment thinking.[1] That was partially correct. Much of the inspiration for the Universal Declaration did indeed come from Enlightenment thinking but there were significant inputs from sources such as the Confucian, Hindu, Islamic and customary traditions. What in fact took place when the Universal Declaration was drafted and adopted was the crystallization of a United Nations philosophy of human rights.

The philosopher, David Hume, grounded morality in human sentiments of mutual solidarity, noted the historical process of the emergence of conventions recording norms for mutual protection, and recognized the role of the Courts in providing protection. These three foundations are very much those of the United Nations philosophy of human rights: sentiments of solidarity,

1 Philosophy, Vol. 92, No. 361, July 2017: Editorial: The Universal Declaration of Human Rights.

conventions, and institutions, albeit incipient, of protection. David Hume would recognize the United Nations philosophy of human rights.

For what has been taking place in the recognition and recording of United Nations human rights norms has been a process in which atrocities, such as the Holocaust, led to the distillation and articulation of human rights norms, insistence on the accountability of governments for upholding these norms, and the development of procedures, institutions and courts for upholding them, to the extent possible, in a still anarchic international order.

The United Nations philosophy of human rights is grounded in the principles of self-determination, good-neighbourliness, friendly relations, and cooperation among nations, which, together, constitute corner-stones of the United Nations Charter. They are buttressed by the principles of mutual respect and tolerance, which are at the heart of the Universal Declaration, as is the principle of equality.

The foundation documents of the United Nations philosophy of human rights are the United Nations Charter, the Universal Declaration of Human Rights, the International Covenant on Civil and Political Rights, the International Covenant on Economic, Social and Cultural Rights, and the Millennium Declaration. The United Nations philosophy of human rights is consensual, customary, cooperative, and inclusive, covering all of humanity.

The United Nations Charter opens with an invocation of 'We the Peoples of the United Nations'. At the time of its adoption, not all of humanity was represented by those who adopted it, but it has subsequently been affirmed by nearly two hundred nations of the world, covering practically all of humanity. 'We the peoples' were, and are, determined to:

> Save succeeding generations from the scourge of war
>
> Reaffirm faith in fundamental human rights, in the dignity and worth of the human person, in the equal rights of men and women, and of nations large and small.
>
> To establish conditions under which justice and respect for the obligations arising from treaties and other sources of international law can be maintained, and
>
> To promote social progress and better standards of life in larger freedom.[2]

2 Preamble to the UN Charter, signed at the United Nations Conference on International organization, San Francisco, California, 26 June,1945.

> To practice tolerance and live together in peace with one another as good neighbours.

The Purposes of the United Nations include:

> To develop friendly relations among nations based on respect for the principle of equal rights and self-determination of peoples, and to take other appropriate measures to strengthen universal peace.
>
> To achieve international cooperation in solving international problems of an economic, social, cultural or humanitarian character, and in promoting and encouraging respect for human rights and for fundamental freedoms for all without distinction as to race, sex, language, or religion.[3]

The United Nations philosophy of human rights is thus grounded in the interrelationship of humanity's quest for peace, development, and human rights. The United Nations has recognized peace as a human right, development as a human right, and a broad range of specific individual and group rights.

The United Nations philosophy of human rights, as reflected in the Millennium Declaration, recognizes that "we have a collective responsibility to uphold the principles of human dignity, equality and equity at the global level."[4] The United Nations, the Millennium Declaration added, considers certain fundamental values to be essential to international relations in the twenty-first century:

> *Freedom*. Men and women have the right to live their lives and raise their children in dignity, free from hunger and from the fear of violence, oppression or injustice. Democratic and participatory governance based on the will of the people best assures these rights.
>
> *Equality*. No individual and no nation must be denied the opportunity to benefit from development. The equal rights and opportunities of women and men must be assured.
>
> *Solidarity*. Global challenges must be managed in a way that distributes the costs and burdens fairly in accordance with basic principles of equity and social justice. Those who suffer or who benefit least deserve help from those who benefit most.

---

3 Article 2 of the Charter.

4 United Nations Millennium Declaration, UN General Assembly resolution 55/2, 13 August, 2001, paragraph 2.

> *Tolerance*. Human beings must respect one another, in all their diversity of belief, culture and language. Differences within and between societies should be neither feared nor repressed, but cherished as a precious asset of humanity. A culture of peace and dialogue among all civilizations should be actively promoted.
>
> *Respect for nature*. Prudence must be shown in the management of all living species and natural resources, in accordance with the precepts of sustainable development. Only in this way can the immeasurable riches provided to us by nature be preserved and passed on to our descendants. The current unsustainable patterns of production and consumption must be changed in the interest of our future welfare and that of our descendants.
>
> *Shared responsibility*. Responsibility for managing worldwide economic and societal development, as well as threats to international peace and security must be shared among the nations of the world and should be exercised multilaterally. As the most universal and most representative organization in the world, the United Nations must play the central role.[5]

While the Universal Declaration of Human Rights refers to the inherency of rights, the process for the elaboration of rights is one of recognition through consensus of the Members of the United Nations. The Declaration opens with the statement that 'recognition of the inherent dignity and of the equal and inalienable rights of all members of the human family is the foundation of freedom, justice and peace in the world.' It goes on to invoke the 'conscience of mankind' and to proclaim that 'the advent of a world in which human beings shall enjoy freedom of speech and belief and freedom from fear and want has been proclaimed as the highest aspiration of the common people.' Human rights should be protected by the rule of law.

The Universal Declaration affirms that everyone is entitled to a social and international order in which human rights and freedoms can be fully realized.[6] Everyone has duties to the community in which alone the free and full development of his or her personality is possible. Addressing the General Assembly at the time of the adoption of the Declaration, the Syrian representative, Mr. Abdul Rahman Kayaly, pleaded: "If there were no social justice, individuals would fight against each other and there would be no peace in the world."[7]

5 Ibid., para.6.

6 Article 28 of the Universal Declaration of Human Rights.

7 A/PV.183, in Schabas, William A., The Universal Declaration of Human Rights. The Travaux Preparatoires. Cambridge, Cambridge University Press, 2013. (3 vols.), pp. 3080 – 3081.

Member States of the United Nations have pledged themselves in the Charter to achieve, in cooperation with the United Nations, the promotion of universal respect for and observance of human rights and fundamental freedoms. The first nine articles of the Universal Declaration of Human Rights[8] have a clear philosophical bent:

> All human beings are born free and equal in dignity and rights. They are endowed with reason and conscience and should act towards one another in a spirit of brotherhood. (Article 1)
>
> Everyone is entitled to all the rights and freedoms set forth in this Declaration without distinction of any kind, such as race, colour, sex, language, religion, political or other opinion, national or social origin, property, birth or other status. (Article 2)
>
> Everyone has the right to life, liberty and security of person (Article 3)
>
> No one shall be held in slavery or servitude; slavery and the slave trade shall be prohibited in all their forms (Article 4)
>
> No one shall be subjected to torture or to cruel, inhuman or degrading treatment or punishment. (Article 5)
>
> Everyone has the right to recognition everywhere as a person before the law (Article 6)
>
> All are equal before the law and are entitled without any discrimination to equal protection of the law. All are entitled to equal protection against any discrimination in violation of this Declaration and against any incitement to such discrimination. (Article 7)
>
> Everyone has the right to an effective remedy by the competent national tribunals for acts violating the fundamental rights granted him/her by the constitution or the law. (Article 8)
>
> No one shall be subjected to arbitrary arrest, detention or exile. (Article 9)

The right to equality is a core tenet of the United Nations philosophy of human rights. The United Nations philosophy of human rights affirms rights that may never be derogated from in any circumstance, such as protection against torture. Protection of the rights of women and of the child is emphasized in the United Nations philosophy of human rights.

The United Nations philosophy of human rights builds on basic rights such as the right to food and the right to health. The need for protection of the poor

8 General Assembly resolution 217 A (III), adopted on 10 December, 1948.

and the vulnerable is recognized in the United Nations philosophy of human rights. The United Nations philosophy of human rights is given expression through efforts for standard-setting, promotion, and protection of human rights. The foundation for these efforts is the International Bill of Rights, which we refer to next.

4 Universality of Human Rights under International Law: The International Bill of Human Rights

The International Bill of Human Rights, which consists of the Universal Declaration of 1948, the International Covenant on Economic, Social and Cultural Rights, and the International Covenant on Civil and Political Rights, both of 1966, highlight the following precepts:

> Society,[as envisaged by Plato], shall be organized for justice (Article 28 of the Universal Declaration)
>
> All human beings are born free and equal in dignity and rights (Article 1 of the Universal Declaration), [recalling Aristotle's reasoning that justice among equals is some form of equality .Unfortunately, Aristotle did not extend equal rights to slaves].
>
> Everyone shall be granted equality before the law and shall be entitled to due process of law.
>
> Everyone should be provided with equal opportunity for a decent life.
>
> Government should strive to prevent violations of human rights and provide remedies and compensation where they have been breached.
>
> Justice shall be provided for the disadvantaged.
>
> Everyone shall be treated humanely and inhumane acts shall be prohibited.
>
> The principle of justice is reinforced by the principle of equity.

At the first meeting of the drafting committee of the former Commission on Human Rights, when it considered the initial draft of a future Universal Declaration, prepared by Professor John Humphrey and the Secretariat, Col. Hodgson (Australia) asked "what was the 'philosophy' behind the paper? What principles did they adopt; what method did they follow? Is it their own idea; is it a collection of various principles?". Humphrey replied that he could not oblige Colonel Hodgson "for the simple reason that [the draft] is based on no philosophy whatsoever." He had been asked to compile a list of rights for discussion purposes, and that was what he had done.[9] A group of philosophers and thinkers assembled at the time by UNESCO to consider the matter, led by Prof. Jacques Maritain, could not come to a philosophical understanding either.

When the plenary Commission on Human Rights began drafting the declaration in 1947, Charles Malik of Lebanon, who was one of the leading philosophers of the Universal Declaration, along with P.C. Chang and Rene Cassin, urged that the Commission base itself on the following four principles:

(a) The human person is more important than the racial, national, or other group to which he may belong;

(b) The human person's most sacred and inviolable possessions are in his mind and his conscience, enabling him to perceive the truth, choose freely, and to exist;

(c) Any social pressure on the part of the state, religion, or race involving the automatic consent of the human person is reprehensible;

(d) The social group to which the individual belongs may, like the human person himself, be wrong or right. The person alone is the judge.[4]

Articles 1 and 2 of the Universal Declaration, building on the human rights provisions of the UN Charter, laid the foundations of the contemporary international legal order and are of the greatest importance legally, philosophically, and from the perspectives of international public policy. The UN General Assembly was effectively announcing to the world that the future governance of humanity must be on the basis of the principles contained in these two articles.

During the discussions in the Commission on Human Rights, when it drafted the Declaration, the Chinese representative, P.C. Chang, commented that Article 1 rested on the basis of eighteenth-century philosophy. That philosophy was based on the innate goodness of man.[10] In declaring human rights for human beings the drafters had sought to protect everyone with human attributes: a thinking being capable of consciousness (experience of thoughts and sensations), with memory, beliefs, hopes and emotions, able to perform actions, which makes them moral agents responsible for what they do.[11]

The drafters, Chang added, were reacting against the Holocaust, grounded in theories of racial superiority, of superior and inferior human beings, and of a

9 Glendon, A World Made New. Eleanor Roosevelt and the Universal Declaration of Human Rights. New York, Random House, (2002), p. 58.

10 A/C.3/ SR 98, reproduced in Schabas, op. cit., p. 2173.

11 See on this S. Mumford, Metaphysics. A Very Short Introduction. Oxford, University Press, 2012, Chapter 7: What is a Person, esp. pp. 65-66.

genocidal campaign against the latter. Protection of peoples from genocide had featured in resolution 96(I) adopted a year before the Universal Declaration and then repeated in the Convention on the Prevention and Punishment of Genocide adopted a day before the Universal Declaration.

Chang would, on many occasions, introduce Confucian concepts into specific articles. He particularly emphasized what he dubbed 'the principle of two-man-mindedness', meaning that we must be ready to see things from one another's point of view. He attached importance to the principle of harmony in the governance of society. It was expressly recognized during the drafting of the declaration that the words "all human beings" had been used precisely in order that both men and women might be included.[12]

When Rene Cassin's refinement of the initial draft by John Humphrey was considered by the Drafting Committee of the Commission, he told it that he had taken two leading ideas as 'fundamental': 'that every human being has a right to be treated like every other human being' and 'the concept of solidarity and fraternity among men.' *Cassin reiterated the point upon which he had insisted since the Commission's very first meeting: the declaration should base universal rights on the 'great fundamental principle of the unity of all the races of mankind'.* Cassin later wrote that the main difficulty in framing the introductory 'General Principles', was "to find a formula that did not require the Commission to take sides on the nature of man and society, or to become immured in metaphysical controversies, notably the conflict among spiritual, rationalist, and materialist doctrines of the origin of human rights.".[13]

The affirmation of human rights for human beings would come to inspire efforts for the protection of minorities, indigenous peoples, children, women and persons with disabilities, among others. The project of the Universal Declaration was one of mutual respect and solidarity for every human being on the planet. This perspective would come to extend recognition of the humanity of tribes and indigenous peoples of all stripes.

The drafters of Articles 1 and 2 of the Universal Declaration sought to register that human beings, by their very nature, should be free to develop to the fullness of their potential, with freedom to think, being in charge of themselves, without being subjected to slavery or subjection, without being in bondage to another, having personal rights and social and political liberty. The concept of freedom was universal, applying to all countries and peoples across the globe,

---

12 A/C.3/SR. 98, reproduced in Schabas, op.cit., p. 2169.

13 Glendon, op.cit., pp. 67-68.

to minority as well as majority populations, to women as well as men, to children, to minorities and indigenous peoples.

On the concept of equality, the factual claim is that human beings are equal; and the normative claim is that human beings should be treated equally. The factual and normative claim, combined, lead to the claim that human beings ought to be treated as the equal beings that they in fact are. Bernard Williams has noted of the idea of equality: *"It is their common humanity that constitutes their equality"*. While the idea of equality has been challenged by some prominent philosophers, such as Robert Nozick, the international community, in the UN Charter, the Universal Declaration, and subsequent normative instruments, has, as a matter of international public policy, elevated the principle of equality into a norm of *jus cogens* in international law.

Kantian ethics had laid stress on the equal right of all human beings to treatment as ends in themselves as a foundation of all morality. During the drafting, Mr. Hernan Santa Cruz (Chile) considered that Article 2 aimed above all at giving expression to one of the basic provisions of the Charter: The United Nations had been founded principally to combat discrimination in the world. It was essential to set forth in a separate article the basic postulates of the declaration, namely the principles of liberty, equality and fraternity.[14] Mr. Ramirez-Moreno of Columbia recognized that the philosophical basis of the phrase 'all human beings are free and equal' was fragile ... It could be alleged that no equality existed, as men were not equally gifted or talented. Human equality, however, should be considered at a deeper level.[15] In other words, this was a matter of international public policy for the future.

The concept of dignity signifies worth, estimation. In modern moral philosophy, especially that of Kant, dignity is considered as a universal attribute, an offshoot of the capacity for self-consciousness and practical reason. The entrenchment of human dignity as a universal human rights norm was one of the great normative innovations of the 1940s. The UN Charter makes several references to the principles of the dignity and equality of all human beings. In the Preamble of the Charter, the Peoples of the United Nations reaffirmed their faith in fundamental rights, in the dignity and worth of the human person and in the equal rights of men and women.

During the drafting of the Universal Declaration, dignity as a right had, at one point, been challenged by the representative of a*partheid* South Africa. Mrs. Roosevelt replied that the word dignity had been considered carefully by

14 A/C.3/SR 100, reproduced in Schabas, op. cit. p. 2196.

15 A/C.3/SR 98, reproduced in Schabas, op. cit.,p. 2171.

the Human Rights Commission, which had included it in order to emphasize that every human being is worthy of respect.[16] The Commission had decided to include it in order to emphasize the inherent dignity of all mankind.[17]

Turning to the concept of a right, Kant thought that the fundamental moral right is to be treated as an end in oneself, and that reason alone justifies and grounds this right. The Charter and the Universal Declaration began a process under which human rights norms are discussed, distilled, and proclaimed in consensual processes by authoritative international organs such as the UN General Assembly. The International Bill of Human Rights and the broader collection of United Nations human rights norms are the outcomes of this process. This, in the stirring words of the late Louis Henkin, is an Age of Rights.[18]

The concept of reason signifies the Intellectual faculty characteristic of human beings by which conclusions are drawn from premises. Among philosophers the concept of reason has attracted a variety of positions. Brand Blanshard's definition of reason, in *Reason and Analysis*,[19] as "the faculty and function of grasping necessary connections" has been considered too narrow.[20] Some consider reason as being the faculty by the exercise of which we can perceive, or arrive, at truths of some particular kind. Reason may signify the careful weighing of arguments and evidence.

The concept of conscience signifies a moral sense of right or wrong as regards things for which one is responsible; a faculty or principle pronouncing upon the moral quality of one's own actions or motives; reason or fairness: the consciousness humans have that an action is morally required or forbidden. As Mr. P.C. Chang put it at one point, "The first condition for defence of the rights of man was tolerance towards the various opinions and beliefs held throughout the world. Uncompromising dogmatism had caused much harm, by accentuating disputes, and lending them an ideological basis ... If harmony was to be maintained in the human community and humanity itself was to be saved, everyone had to accept, in a spirit of sincere tolerance, the different views and beliefs of his fellow men. By pleading for tolerance of all opinions and beliefs and by insisting on precision of terminology, the Chinese delegation had striven to introduce certain improvements into the universal declaration of human rights."[21]

---

16 Glendon, op. cit.,p. 146.

17 A/C.3/SR 98, reproduced in Schabas, op. cit., p. 2169.

18 L. Henkin, The Age of Rights. New York, Columbia University Press,1990.

19 Brand Blanshard, Reason and Analysis. London, 1962.

20 G.J. Warnock,"Reason", in The Encyclopedia of Philosophy. Paul Edwards, Editor in Chief, London, Macmillan, 1967, Vol. 7, pp. 83-85.

21 A/PV. 182, reproduced in Schabas, op. cit. p. 3058.

The concept of brotherhood signifies fraternal tie. During the drafting process, Mr. Kayali (Syria), commented that the word brotherhood was an expression of the ideal moral relationship which should exist between human beings and meant that everyone should behave to others as they would wish others to behave to them.[22] Mr. Anze Matienzo (Bolivia), thought that there was no intention of claiming that human beings were perfect. The draft declaration was designed to set a goal for mankind. It should inspire men to transform into realities the principles it proclaimed.[23]

Mr. Chang (China) commented that the second sentence of Article 1 called upon men to act towards one another in a spirit of brotherhood. That attitude was perfectly consistent with the Chinese attitude towards manners and the importance of kindly and considerate treatment of others. It was only when man's social behaviour rose to that level that he was truly human. Decorum was an ideal which should not be lost sight of – as unfortunately it was – in the struggle to uphold noble principles.[24] Mr. Pavlov (USSR) (USSR) thought that a real spirit of brotherhood was possible only in the absence of exploitation of man by man.

The United Nations philosophy of human rights, as recapitulated above, provides the indispensable basis for international cooperation for the welfare of all of humanity. As we write, one can see various assertions among contending powers: sovereign rights, party-led democracy, religious claims about the bases of governance, and dictatorial assertions from various quarters. They must all face the conscience of humanity, which is grounded in the United Nations philosophy of human rights, carefully developed over the past decades.

Notwithstanding the foregoing solid foundations of universality in international law, the concept is actively under challenge from powerful governments, as we shall relate next.

5 Challenges to Universality

In politics and academia, great debates continue to rage over the universality of human rights.[2] Some contend that human rights are not universal, arguing rather for cultural relativism in applying human rights norms. Some have argued for the primacy of religious tenets over international human rights

22 A/C.3/SR 99, reproduced in Schabas, op. cit., p. 2184.

23 A/C.3/SR 98, reproduced in Schabas, op. cit., p. 2173.

24 A/C.3/SR 96, reproduced in Schabas, op. cit., p. 2152.

norms. As will be demonstrated later in this chapter, these arguments are flawed.

In June 2016, China and Russia issued joint statements on strengthening global strategic stability, developing legal regulation of information security and cybersecurity, and promoting international law. The Declaration of the Russian Federation and the People's Republic of China on the Promotion of International law (Joint Declaration) sets out principles to guide these two states in their approach to international law. As Lauri Malksoo has observed:

> [I]n adopting it, China and Russia appeared to be seeking to present a united challenge to Western hegemony in international law. ...
>
> These principles are mutual respect for sovereignty and territorial integrity, mutual nonaggression, non-interference in each other's internal affairs, equality and mutual benefit, and peaceful coexistence; they do not include any mention of human rights.
>
> This emphasis on state sovereignty over human rights is a hallmark of many Chinese, and of some Russian, statements on international law. ...[25]

Furthermore, Malksoo commented:

> In post-Soviet international law scholarship in Russia, human rights is a subject treated with great interest and sometimes even enthusiasm but it is nevertheless subjugated to the principle of state sovereignty.[26]

In the UN Human Rights Council in 2009. Russia sponsored a resolution calling for a study on the contribution traditional values can make to human rights promotion. This initiative and outcome reflected the influential thought-world of the Russian Orthodox Church and its Patriarch Kirill I. The European states and the US voted against the resolution but it was nevertheless adopted by a narrow margin.[27]

Xue Hanqin, a Chinese Judge on the International Court of Justice, has argued:

25 Anthea Roberts, Is International Law International? New York, Oxford University Press, 2018, pp. 190-191.

26 Lauri Malksoo, Russian Approaches to International Law .Oxford University Press, 2015., p. 125.

27 Ibid, p. 166.

> China's position on cultural relativism is not intended to challenge Western values and its liberal rights models, but to argue that these models and values are not the only way to promote and protect human rights.[28]

The promotion of human rights, Judge Hanqin noted, is both a cause and a process. This means that as an objective for social progress, human rights should be relentlessly pursued at all times. As part of social development, nevertheless, human rights progress is a long process. Individual rights and freedoms cannot be substantiated without particular social conditions, nor can they be taken out of social context for examination.[29]

Judge Hanqin explained that in promoting human rights, China has adhered to a number of basic principles:

- First, China is of the view that the human rights cause should be promoted in line with each State's social and economic development. In reality, social factors as such often prove to be more relevant and decisive for the realization of human rights. China believes that as a social movement, human rights promotion should proceed in a gradual and incremental fashion. In principle, human right protection remains in relative terms for every country, subject to the level and degree of its development.
- Secondly, while accepting universality and inseparability of human rights, China attaches importance to economic, social and cultural rights and the right to development in its human rights process. China is of the view that the essential task for most developed countries at this stage is first and foremost to pursue economic and social development. China's view is shared by Asian countries as enunciated in the Bangkok Declaration adopted by Asian countries in 1993. China's position accords precedence of economic and social rights over civil and political rights.
- Thirdly, China also emphasizes the correlation between the human rights cause and the rule of law. In promoting rights and freedoms, as a corollary, China lays stress on duties and obligations of citizens under the rule of law.
- Fourthly, in promoting international protection of human rights, China advocates mutual respect, non-interference, non-confrontational and constructive dialogues. It opposes the double standards practised against the developing world. China considers that the Universal Periodic Review was

28 Xue Hanqin, Chinese Contemporary Perspectives on International Law., History, Culture and International Law. Hague Academy of International Law 2012.

29 Ibid, p. 120.

created to ensure equal treatment for every country when human rights situations are assessed at national level.[30]

On the international protection of human rights, China, according to Judge Hanqin, recognizes that its engagement in efforts for international protection has facilitated its domestic efforts on human rights and the rule of law. International dialogues in the human rights field at various levels have promoted academic studies on rights issues at home and accelerated its legislative process on the protection of citizens' rights.[31]

China is of the view that human rights dialogues in international relations are often conducted with certain political and ideological preferences. China has adopted a different approach from the West towards human rights protection. China's is aware that its adherence to collective culturalism and social rights is sometimes perceived as a challenge to Western values and liberal human rights models. China had noted that when the human rights performance of developing countries is being evaluated, external assessment tended to be based on 'standardized' criteria of the developed world.

China is of the view that in human rights discourse, the sequencing debate, namely, whether the establishment of the rule of law and a functional legal system should precede democratization is not merely a theoretical issue. In China's view, as a social cause, human rights improvements not only rely on accumulation and allocation of wealth, but also needs time, often a long time for gradual and incremental social progress to take place.

In a telling observation, Judge Hanqin commented:

> The difference between universalism and cultural relativism should not be deemed a rivalry to the West if the human rights cause is taken seriously and the interests of the people are placed in the centre of the debate. China's position on cultural relativism is not intended to challenge Western values and its liberal rights models, but to argue that these values and models are not the *only* way to promote and protect human rights. They may be suitable and perfect for Western countries as their history and culture have proved, but they may not suit as well other countries with different historical and cultural backgrounds. To require other countries to immediately realize what Western countries have taken hundreds of years to do cannot simply be taken as politically naïve …

30 Ibid., p. 149.ff.

31 Ibid., p. 160 ff.

> [S]houldn't we ask ourselves what are the real objectives of human rights? What is the responsibility of the international community?
>
> The rapid transformation from the planned economy to market economy in the most populous country has given rise to many new challenges to China in the human rights field. China takes human rights seriously. It does so not for others but for the well-being of its own people. In pursuing its social and economic development goals, China will continue its efforts in promoting human rights protection, both domestically and internationally.[32]

On the right to development, Judge Hanqin noted that it remains a challenging issue for each and every country, developed and developing alike. It is both a development issue as well as a rights theme. Human development in harmony with its environmental and natural conditions is a goal that requires our persistent pursuit for a balance between development and environment, for in our hands we hold the happiness of the present and future generations on this one and common planet.[33]

Congyan Cai, has pertinently noted that "An acceptance of human rights is indispensable for a state in the process of rising as a great power in the era of human rights. On the other hand, China seeks to insulate its executive authority from international pressure by neutralizing the application of human rights treaties in the judiciary. In practice, China disallows the automatic incorporation of treaties under which executive authority might be seriously challenged. As a result, China's executive branch can take advantage of the supposed socialist 'efficiency' advantage. The 2014 amendment of the APL demonstrates that China remains reluctant to allow the application of international law in its domestic courts."[34]

A search that Prof. Cai conducted "did not reveal any cases in which Chinese courts gave direct effect to human rights treaties, which constitute the core of this kind of legal relationship and are crucial to enhancing the rule of law, especially in transitional states."[35]

---

32 Ibid, p. 165.

33 Ibid., p. 208.

34 Congyan Cai, "International Law in Chinese Courts during the Rise of China", in Anthea Roberts et. el., Comparative International Law. New York, Oxford University Press, 2018, pp. 295-318, at p. 314.

35 Ibid., p. 312.

6 Defending Universality

Some years ago, the late Senator José Diokno of the Philippines summarily dispatched arguments about cultural diversity that sought to diminish universality:

> "Two justifications for authoritarianism in Asian developing countries are currently fashionable ... One is that Asian societies are authoritarian and paternalistic and so need governments that are also authoritarian and paternalistic; that Asia's hungry masses are too concerned with filling their stomachs to concern themselves with civil liberties and political freedoms; that the Asian conception of freedom differs from that of the West; that, in short, Asians are not fit for human rights.
>
> "Another is that developing countries must sacrifice freedom temporarily to achieve the rapid economic development that their exploding populations and rising expectations demand; in short, that governments must be authoritarian to promote development.
>
> "Well, the first justification is racist nonsense. And I will say no more than that. The second is a lie: authoritarianism is not needed for development; what it is needed for is to maintain the status quo.
>
> Regardless ... of what dictators and social scientists may say, we Asians know that the loss of freedom does not lead to a better life. On the contrary, we know that life cannot become better – it cannot even be good – unless people are free".[3]

6.1 *The Democratic Test of Universality*

There is an irrefutable democratic test that confirms the concept of the universality of rights. It is a simple matter. Just ask any human being: Would you like to live or be killed arbitrarily? Would you like to be tortured or enslaved? Would you like to live free or be in prison? Would you like to be in bondage? Would you like to have a say in how you are governed? The democratic test of universality is the basis for its strongest affirmation.[17]

6.2 *The Bases of Universality*

The bases of the universality of human rights are: (1) all human beings claim their inherent human rights; (2) the common humanity of all human beings and the inherency of rights; (3) the formal affirmation and reaffirmation of human rights in consensual processes of authoritative decision-making bodies such as the UN General Assembly and world conferences on human rights.

There may, indeed, be discussion about whether every internationally proclaimed human right is universal or if global consensus is lacking regarding a particular asserted right. There was in the past for example, a lively debate about the right to change one's religion or belief. This right was included in the Universal Declaration but not in the International Covenant on Civil and Political Rights and it was fudged in the 1992 Declaration on Freedom of Religion or Belief. Where a particular human right is contested by one or more government or group, the matter must be assessed by referring to the tests of inherency and consensus.

When a right is contested, recourse may be had to the principle of inherency, namely that one should enjoy certain rights from the very nature of one's common humanity. The example of the right to change one's religion or belief was referred to above. One can understand religions or laws prohibiting religious proselytizing or forbidding campaigns to convince people to change their religion. But if an individual decides to change her or his religion or belief, how can this be forbidden by any religion or law? The universality of the right to change one's religion or belief would therefore rest in the principle of inherency.

There are repeated instances of the reaffirmation of consensus over the universality of human rights in authoritative fora of the international community such as the Vienna World Conference on Human Rights, the Millennium Declaration, and the outcome document of the Summit of World Leaders in 2005.

The Vienna conference reaffirmed all states' solemn commitment to fulfill their obligations to promote universal respect for, observance of, and protection of all human rights and fundamental freedoms in accordance with the UN Charter, other instruments relating to human rights, and international law. In ringing terms, it proclaimed that: "The universal nature of these rights and freedoms is beyond question."[18]

The Millennium Declaration reaffirmed the UN's commitment to the Charter's purposes and principles, "which have proved timeless and universal. Indeed, their relevance and capacity to inspire have increased, as nations and peoples have become increasingly interconnected and interdependent." It pledged: "We resolve … to respect fully and uphold the Universal Declaration of Human Rights; to strive for the full protection and promotion in all our countries of civil, political, economic, social and cultural rights for all."

The General Assembly considered certain fundamental values essential to international relations in the twenty-first century. These included: freedom, equality, solidarity, tolerance, respect for nature, and shared responsibility.

The Summit of World Leaders in 2005 reaffirmed the centrality of human rights in the UN's work and endorsed the responsibility to protect.[21] The world leaders declared their readiness to refer genocide, ethnic cleansing, crimes against humanity, and war crimes to the UN Security Council.

6.3 *Challenges of Implementation*

It has been argued that the universality of human rights is belied by the fact that these rights are not respected in practice or are grossly violated in large parts of the world. Lack of implementation is certainly a feature of our contemporary world. So are gross violations of human rights. But this is not an argument against universality. In national legal systems, the validity of laws is not belied by the fact that many are breached. This is an issue of law and order and protection.

An individual's rights are not taken away because they are not respected or are violated. This is a challenge of universal implementation and protection that the entire international human rights movement is striving to address.

6.4 *Normative Universality*

Authoritative organs of the international community, such as the General Assembly, the World Conference on Human Rights (1993), and the UN Human Rights Council have repeatedly reaffirmed the universality of human rights. The UN Millennium Declaration recognized a set of fundamental values for the twenty-first century.

6.5 *Universality in the UN Human Rights Council: The UPR Process*

All 193 States Members of the UN participating in the Universal Periodic Review Process of the Human Rights Council formally state their adherence to the universality of human rights. Practice on the ground, however, is quite different in numerous countries.

6.6 *Political Universality*

Notwithstanding their participation in the reaffirmation of normative universality, some major powers emphasize 'sovereign rights' over individual rights while some prefer to play by their own rules. There is a challenge here to the universality of instruments such as the Universal Declaration of Human Rights.

6.7 *The Universality of International Law*

In the contemporary literature one finds some voices even raising questions about the universality of international law itself.

6.8 *Populism and Universality*

In an era of populism, many governments make up their own standards, in direct breach of the universal standards. Universality on the ground is thus under stress

6.9 *Global Poverty and Universality*

Even if Governments formally reaffirm the universality of human rights, millions of people in the world suffer from grievous poverty. Universality floats above their heads in these circumstances.

6.10 *Gross Violations of Human Rights and Universality*

Gross violations of human rights are rampant in numerous parts of the world. Here, again, universality is in the air above the heads of the victims.

6.11 *Democratic Universality/Peoples' Universality*

This is the acid test of universality: as we noted earlier in this chapter, if people on the ground, throughout the world, were given the chance to express their views, they would reaffirm the universality of human rights: they would choose freedom from enslavement, torture, arbitrary imprisonment, and inequality. The democratic test of universality provides the strongest basis for its reaffirmation.

The thread running through the history of human rights is one of human societies cross-fertilizing and learning from one another, converging toward a great synthesis around binding international human rights norms. Viewed from this perspective, the universality of rights has been authoritatively affirmed in the international community, and there is a formal consensus on universality.

The universality of human rights must be vigorously upheld. It rests on the idea that there is a minimum body of basic human rights that belongs to every human being regardless of his or her country of origin or philosophical, religious, or other beliefs. Regional or national charters may add to the universal body of human rights but may not detract from them.

The validity of the universality of human rights is not lessened by the fact that, in practice, human rights are violated in many parts of the world. But rights exist even if they are breached, and the challenge is to work for their implementation and protection.

6.12 *Universality as an Idea*

The concept of human rights has developed over the centuries and has roots in all of the major world religions. In turn, these principles have been codified in international legal instruments, namely the Universal Declaration of Human Rights (UDHR). Since its proclamation in 1948, the UDHR has been re-endorsed in international and regional treaties and in authoritative policy pronouncements by governments and people in Africa, the Americas, Asia, and Europe. This certainly underscores the universality of human rights.

6.13 *Universality as a Goal*

If human beings have so many things in common, is it strange to want to preserve these common characteristics and to reach out in mutual support and cooperation? Can we protect the environment or keep the air clean unless we do so together? Is it wrong to say that every human being should have an equal opportunity to develop his or her potential? Is universality then not valid as a goal for common aspirations?

The idea that all human beings at the beginning of the twenty-first century possess, as part of their birthright, a core of inalienable rights is not disputed. What is sometimes debated is the content of particular rights and the need for change. This is a legitimate debate. The international human rights treaties inspired by the UDHR contain amendment procedures that could deal with claims for modernization or updating. The UDHR, however, stands on its own as a historic, inspirational document. The universality of core human rights is quite compatible with cultural diversity, and the argument of cultural diversity should not challenge the core universal human rights but, rather, might influence the mode and manner of their application in particular societies. One can, for example, proclaim freedom of religion or belief, while leaving it to each person to choose a religion or belief. The notion of good faith in applying universal human rights norms comes into the picture here.

The existence of duties does not negate the universality of human rights. Rather, as is explicitly recognized in article 29 of the UDHR, everyone has duties to his or her community. That same article further states that one may be subject only to such limitations as determined by law in the exercise of rights and freedoms. Such limitations may only be for the purpose of securing due recognition and respect for the rights and freedoms of others and of meeting the requirements of morality, public order, and general welfare.

6.14 *Universality as a Normative Concept*

In the history of the international community, has it not been found necessary to postulate universal norms? And have the norms not been useful? Is not the very notion of international law grounded in the concept of a law applicable to all communities – at least in respect of imperative norms of public policy (*jus cogens*) and international customary law? Would order be possible in the international community without a system of norms of universal applicability and validity? The answer can only be in the negative. That being the case, is it not entirely natural and proper that the stock of norms of international law would also include norms of universal human rights?

By the very act of joining the organization, all UN member states commit to the principle of universality contained in the Charter and the UDHR. The commitment to universality is itself universal. When the Commission on Human Rights began drafting the UDHR in 1947, Charles Malik of Lebanon urged that the commission base itself on the following four principles:

(a) the human person is more important than the racial, national, or other group to which he may belong;
(b) the human person's most sacred and inviolable possessions are in his mind and his conscience, enabling him to perceive the truth, choose freely, and to exist;
(c) any social pressure on the part of the state, religion, or race involving the automatic consent of the human person is reprehensible;
(d) the social group to which the individual belongs may, like the human person himself, be wrong or right. The person alone is the judge.

The spirit animating the drafting committee members is inspiring to read, even seven and a half decades later. At an early drafting session, Rene Cassin proposed that two or three fundamental principles be incorporated in the outline:

(a) the unity of the human race or family;
(b) the idea that every human being has a right to be treated like every other human being;
(c) the concept of solidarity and fraternity among men.

Hernán Santa Cruz of Chile opined that the drafting committee must draw up a charter of human rights, giving it not only legal but real human content. He further suggested that this charter should be a spiritual guide for humanity, enumerating the rights that must be respected everywhere.

The UDHR's opening article was significantly influenced by Asia. During the second session of the drafting committee, on 5 December 1947, Carlos Romulo of the Philippines proposed to redraft article 1 as discussed in the first session in June 1947 on the basis of Cassin's draft proposal. In response, the chairman invited the French and Philippine representatives to submit a new text of the article. At the ninth meeting of the drafting committee, on 10 December 1947, Romulo proposed the following text: "All men are brothers. Being endowed by nature with reason and conscience, they are born free and possess equal dignity and rights."

Following further discussion, the following text proposed by the Philippines and France was adopted: "All men are born free and equal in dignity and rights.

They are endowed with reason and conscience and should act towards one another like brothers." With some subsequent polishing, the following is what was adopted as the UDHR's opening article: "All human beings are born free and equal in dignity and rights. They are endowed with reason and conscience and should act towards one another in a spirit of brotherhood."

The Egyptian representative, Osman Obeid, made a case for including a mention of individuals' duties as a corollary to his or her rights. He made the following stirring plea for justice for the peoples of the world: "The principles of human rights should be set forth in clear terms. The peoples of the world would greet with enthusiasm the first action taken by the United Nations to enforce redressment of wrongs."

Representatives from Africa, Asia, the Americas, and Europe thus influenced the drafting of the UDHR. In the drafting process, detailed draft declarations were submitted by Chile, Cuba, and Panama. In compiling materials from all over the globe to aid in drafting the declaration, the secretariat drew on the constitutions and legislation of 55 countries from Africa, Asia, Latin America, and Eastern Europe. Only 14 were from Western countries.

Developing countries also were actively involved. The Philippines proposed an article stating that everyone had the right to participate in their government, both directly or indirectly, through elections that are periodic, free, and conducted by secret ballot. The Panamanian representative proposed an article declaring that the state has a duty to maintain comprehensive arrangements to promote health, prevent sickness and accident, and provide medical care and compensation for the loss of livelihood.

Malik argued that social and economic rights and the problem of discrimination were very important and should form part of the instrument. P C. Chang of China called for a document that would accord with the spirit and atmosphere of the post-war era and argued that the document should reflect freedom from want. India tabled a draft declaration that included the following statement: "Every human being has the right of equality, without distinction of race, sex, language, religion, nationality or political belief."

This is a mere sampling of the defining contributions of the representatives from Africa, Asia, and Latin America in drafting the UDHR. At the World Conference on Human Rights in 1993, the representatives, assembled from around the world, reaffirmed the universality of human rights in the most emphatic terms.

The UDHR has inspired regional instruments to protect human rights throughout the globe, all of which have reaffirmed its precepts. This may be seen in the constitution of the OAU (now the African Union), the African Charter on Human and People's Rights, the Arab Charter on Human Rights, the

Cairo Islamic Declaration on Human Rights, the LAWASIA Statement of Basic Principles of Human Rights, the American Convention on Human Rights, and the European Convention on Human Rights. These endorsements of the UDHR bear witness to its universal status.

7 Conclusion

During his tenure, UN Secretary-General Kofi Annan had to deal with numerous crises, conflicts, and governance problems in Africa. He had to contend with assertions by some African leaders that international human rights norms were foreign impositions and did not correspond to African culture and realities. He met these challenges head on during an address to the OAU summit in Harare on 2 June 1997. He declared:

> [L]et us dedicate ourselves to a new doctrine for African politics: where democracy has been usurped let us do whatever is in our power to restore it to its rightful owners, the people.
>
> Verbal condemnation, though necessary and desirable, is not sufficient. We must also ostracize and isolate putschists
>
> The success of Africa's third wave depends equally on respect for fundamental human rights. The conflicts which have disfigured our continent have all too often, been accompanied by massive human rights violations.
>
> Africa can no longer tolerate and accept as *faits accomplis,* coups against elected governments, and the illegal seizure of power by military cliques. I am aware of the fact that some view this concern as a luxury of the rich countries for which Africa is not ready. I know that others treat it as an imposition, if not a plot, by the industrialized west. I find these thoughts truly demeaning, demeaning of the yearning for human dignity that resides in every African heart.
>
> Do not African mothers weep when their sons or daughters are killed or maimed by agents of repressive rule? Are not African fathers saddened when their children are unjustly jailed or tortured? Is not Africa as a whole impoverished when even one of its brilliant voices is silenced?
>
> We cannot afford to lose one life, spare one idea, relinquish one hope, if we are to succeed on our chosen course. So I say this to you, my brothers and sisters, that human rights are African rights, and I call upon you to ensure that all Africans are able fully to enjoy them.

> Let us work together and with the United Nations to develop good governance and respect for the rule of law. When we succeed, Africa will have taken a great step forward.

Let us reiterate: there is a simple democratic test of universality. If any human being is asked whether she or he would like to be free from arbitrary and summary execution, torture, arbitrary arrest and detention, enforced or involuntary disappearance, and persecution on grounds of religion or belief, there can be no doubt that every human being would answer in the positive. From this, we may conclude that there is a basic set of fundamental human rights that all human beings would claim, affirm, and defend.

CHAPTER 3

Protection

1 Introduction

Without a doubt, there is activity within the Human Rights Council that aims at the protection of human rights. Nevertheless, the Council has come in for heavy criticism on the ground that, for political reasons, it fails to take principled action in respect of many situations of gross violations of human rights. In this chapter, we will, among other things, reproduce an extensive report from the UN High Commissioner for Human Rights detailing gross violations of human rights in more than fifty countries. Did the Council act on this appeal to conscience? Alas, the evidence, for the most part, is 'no'. The protection record of the Council is, to say the least, spotty.

The protection of human rights has three key components: preventive, reactive, curative. UN norms prescribe ground rules for all Governments on how they must protect human rights. The foundation of these norms includes the Universal Declaration and the International Covenants. These are universal norms applicable to all countries.

Inspired by, and reflecting the international norms, every country should have in place an adequate and effective national protection system. This includes constitutional provisions reflecting the Universal Declaration and the Covenants, legislative provisions reflecting international human rights treaties accepted by the Government, judicial enforcement of human rights, a national human rights institution charged with promoting and protecting human rights, education and dissemination of human rights, and arrangements to help prevent violations of human rights from taking place. International protection becomes necessary when these measures of national protection fail to safeguard human rights within a country.

2 Efforts for International Protection

The development of international protection is still at an early stage, notwithstanding that efforts have been under way since the establishment of the United Nations in 1945. The Universal Periodic Review, which is operated by the UN Human Rights Council, can help countries develop or enhance their national protection systems. It can also provide an opportunity to air concerns

 | DOI:10.1163/9789004504950_005

about human rights problems within a country. NGOs can make written submissions into the process. To a limited extent, they are also able to take the floor in the plenary of the Human Rights Council.

The Special Procedures of the UN Human Rights Council are the strongest protection actors within the United Nations. They investigate and publish reports about human rights problems such as extra-judicial executions, torture, enforced and involuntary disappearances, racism and racial discrimination, violence against women, trafficking in human beings and similar problems. The Special Procedures can also issue urgent appeals where people are at risk of imminent violations of their human rights.

There is an international complaints procedure that NGOs can activate by submitting reliably attested information about gross violations of human rights. Unfortunately, it is heavily politicised by Governments, which control it inside the Human Rights Council. But NGOs should be aware of it so that they can consider using it by submitting complaints about allegations of gross violations of human rights.

There are some individual petitions procedures established under particular treaties, which complainants may be able to use. Prominent among these is the procedure under the Optional Protocol to the Covenant on Civil and Political Rights. There is a rich international jurisprudence that has been developed from the case law of the human rights treaty bodies.

Several prominent international human rights NGOs operate at the United Nations and they help advance the protection of human rights at the United Nations. These include Amnesty International, Human Rights Watch, the International Commission of Jurists, the International Service for Human Rights, and Geneva for Human Rights.

The UN Secretary-General, the High Commissioner for Human Rights, and the President of the UN Human Rights Council are international personalities of moral stature who help publicise and respond to human rights causes. We refer to the Human Rights Council itself below.

The Social and Humanitarian Committee of the UN General Assembly sometimes discusses human rights problems inside countries. NGOs are not allowed to speak in the Committee but their concerns can be raised by a Government or Governments. The prominent international human rights NGOs can help in briefing governmental representatives on the Committee about human rights problems that deserve United Nations attention.[1]

1 See generally, Julie Mertus, The UN and Human Rights. London, Routledge, 2008.

3 The Human Rights Council

The UN Human Rights Council discusses and prepares new human rights norms. It tries to promote human rights generally. Its record of actually protecting human rights is not even-handed because of political influences of Governments. It can be used as a forum to help air grievances and to publicise violations. NGOs are given limited space to speak in the Council but they can organise parallel meetings to help air their grievances. The Human Rights Council is essentially a political body and often does not act on the principle of justice. Rather, it acts for the most part on the basis of political expediency. The Council meets in three sessions per year and sometimes holds special sessions to discuss human rights emergencies. The Council has a record of establishing international commissions of inquiry when it is faced with situations of severe violations of human rights.

The Human Rights Council performs a valuable role as a forum for airing grievances about gross violations of human rights world-wide. The updates provided by the UN High Commissioner for Human Rights to each session of the Council are an example of this. We relate below the High Commissioner's update to the Council in February, 2021.

4 High Commissioner's Updates to the Human Rights Council on Situations of Concern

At the 46th session of the Human Rights Council, on 26 February, 2021, High Commissioner Michele Bachelet provided the following update to the Council on situations of concern in some fifty countries. This is a stunning example of an effort to generate protection within the Council for victims of gross violations of human rights world-wide.

> 26 February 2021
>
> Excellencies, Colleagues and friends,
>
> The leaders of countries are called to make many difficult decisions in the turbulence of today's events. To address the multiple challenges of COVID-19, in terms of health policies; sudden economic crises and financial shortfalls; and the rising distress of people from every walk of life is an immense and challenging task. I am convinced, by my own experience and the lessons of history, that the best way to approach such dilemmas is to involve the public. In their diversity of views, experiences and needs, a country's people are its leader's finest and most important resource.

Participation is a right – and it is also a means that ensures better, more effective policy. To help heal harms, bridge deep fractures, and lead change that meets expectations, every society, and every leader, needs to engage the public's participation, fully and meaningfully. All over the world, people clearly manifest their rightful demand to have a role in shaping policy. Acting on that demand is the only way to build public trust – and it is also the best way to drive policies that are based on lived realities and made better by frank and constant feedback.

I draw your attention to the *UN Guidance Note on protecting and promoting civic space*, which makes it clear why maintaining and expanding civic freedoms is central to the UN's efforts across all pillars, including development and peace. COVID-19 has demonstrated – once again – how urgent and vital this work is for States, as well as multilateral institutions.

It is precisely at this time of crisis that solid public participation; official accountability through oversight institutions and a free press are most needed, to devise policies that can navigate shocks most effectively. This is a time for more, not less, transparency; for more information; for more public debate and discussion, in a more open and inclusive civic space; and for more responsive governance, which more firmly upholds human rights.

Madam President, the situations in Afghanistan, Belarus, Central African Republic, Colombia, Cyprus, the Democratic People's Republic of Korea, the Democratic Republic of Congo, Eritrea, Guatemala, Honduras, Nicaragua, the Occupied Palestinian Territory, Sri Lanka, Ukraine and Venezuela will be discussed at other meetings during this session.

Excellencies,

In the Russian Federation, I regret the entry into force late last year of new legal provisions which further limit fundamental freedoms, including the constitutionally guaranteed rights to free expression, peaceful assembly and association. Existing restrictive laws have continued to be harshly enforced, including during recent demonstrations across the country. On several occasions, police were filmed using unnecessary and disproportionate force against largely peaceful protesters, and made thousands of arrests. I also note with concern the growing expansion of the definition of 'foreign agent'.

In Turkey, the newly passed Law No. 7262, with the stated aim of preventing financing of weapons of mass destruction, introduces more restrictions and oversight on civil society organisations. Its application – together with the social media bill adopted last July, and other restrictive legislation – could further increase the use of vaguely defined terrorism charges to target and silence perceived critics. Reprisals against people who seek justice and accountability – including for the victims of enforced disappearances – are compounding the erosion of judicial independence and rule of law, and contribute to an increasingly unsafe civic environment. Crackdowns on student-led protests underline the need for greater dialogue with many constituencies. I am also concerned about last week's raids and mass arrests, including of opposition members, allegedly in connection with terrorism related charges. Any anti-terror operation should comply with international human rights law, and should not be used to target dissent.

In Kazakhstan, I am dismayed by recent administrative prosecutions of NGOs. While suspensions have been lifted, the penalties for alleged inaccuracies in the filing of administrative records on foreign funding appear to be disproportionate and aimed at obstructing their work. I call the authorities to amend national legislation and to eliminate these far-reaching reporting requirements, which have impact on the right to freedom of association.

I welcome the cessation of hostilities in the Nagorno-Karabakh conflict zone, which was announced by the leaders of Azerbaijan, Armenia and the Russian Federation in their joint trilateral statement on 9 November. I call for investigations into all alleged serious violations of international law that occurred in and around Nagorno-Karabakh. It is essential to ensure accountability of those responsible, and redress for the victims. I welcome criminal proceedings launched by Azerbaijan into the activities of four members of the Azerbaijan armed forces. I remind all States that all captured or detained persons should be treated humanely, and benefit from the protections of international law. I continue to seek access for my Office.

I am concerned that measures taken by several European countries are restricting the work of organisations that protect migrants' rights, and deliver them life-saving assistance. A recent update by the EU Fundamental Rights Agency has identified some 50 criminal or administrative proceedings initiated by Germany, Greece, Italy, Malta, the Netherlands and Spain since 2016, against humanitarian actors involved in search and rescue in the Mediterranean. Most have been in Italy, and the majority have occurred since 2019. We understand that only four humanitarian ships are currently operational in the Central Mediterranean, while several others have been impounded or prevented from operating – raising grave concerns about people's safety on one of the deadliest migration routes in the world. My Office has repeatedly expressed our concerns regarding such measures, as well as related acts of intimidation, harassment, obstruction or denial of access.

In Hungary, the Government has criminalized the provision of assistance to migrants, as well as the organization of border monitoring, thus denying access to civil society to monitor reports of violent pushbacks and other serious human rights violations at the EU's external borders. I am seriously concerned that Hungarian police have carried out some 5,000 pushbacks to Serbia in the last two months alone, in breach of Hungary's international human rights obligations as well as EU law.

In Croatia, the authorities have sought to hinder public scrutiny of migration practices by denying access to the ombudswoman and human rights organisations, and discrediting their reports. Last month, the Croatian authorities blocked Members of the European Parliament from visiting border areas with Bosnia and Herzegovina, amid credible allegations of human rights violations.

Civil society and independent monitoring are fundamental to the health of all societies. I encourage the European Union and Member States to ensure that this trend of shrinking civic space is reversed, and to establish adequate protections, including through the EU Pact on Asylum and Migration.

Madam President,

The pandemic has sharpened and shifted our view of what is valuable in any country's economy. Health-care, child-care and social protections are now viewed as essential and effective instruments, which pay high dividends in warding off devastating economic pain. And yet many countries in Asia and the Pacific spend less than 2 per cent of GDP on social protection – compared with the global average of 11 per cent – and large parts of the economy remain informal. I encourage action across the region to achieve far more comprehensive social protection systems – including for migrants – as a core component of plans to recover on a healthy and sustainable foundation.

Across Southeast Asia, there has been a serious contraction in civic space. This Council discussed the alarming situation in Myanmar earlier this month. In Cambodia, Indonesia – including in the Papua region – Thailand and Vietnam, people have gathered peacefully to call for Governments to uphold rights and to implement democratic principles of accountability, transparency, participation and the rule of law. In response, many activists, human rights defenders, environmental actors and journalists have been subjected to arbitrary detention and arrest, harassment and violence, and have faced highly punitive criminal charges and sentences. In all these countries, as well as Lao PDR and the Philippines, we have also documented the arrests and detentions of individuals for exercising the right to free expression, including online. Restrictive legislation on social media, and vaguely worded prohibitions of what is termed "fake news" have been used to silence people, including health-workers and others who report on COVID in their hospitals and neighbourhoods.

I am particularly concerned about the severe shrinking of civic space in Cambodia, where increasing and disproportionate legislative and administrative measures limit the rights to free expression, peaceful assembly, association and information, among others.

In the Philippines, we are working with a range of partners to implement this Council's recent resolution. A UN joint programme on human rights is being finalized, and I will continue to urge the genuine and meaningful participation of all possible constituencies so that it can deliver effective results. The continued high number of killings by police remain a serious concern.

In India, continued protests by hundreds of thousands of farmers highlight the importance of ensuring laws and policies are based on meaningful consultations with those concerned. I trust that ongoing dialogue efforts by both sides will lead to an equitable solution to this crisis that respects the rights of all. Charges of sedition against journalists and activists for reporting or commenting on the protests, and attempts to curb freedom of expression on social media, are disturbing departures from essential human rights principles. With regard to inclusion and participation, I am encouraged by the recent experience of my Office in a pilot programme in Kerala State, where officials, civil society organisations and community leaders have used innovative technology to ensure that the voices of marginalized and poor people are heard, and their needs addressed, in the pandemic response.

We continue to monitor the situation in Indian-administered Kashmir, where restrictions on communications, and clampdowns on civil society activists, remain of concern. Despite recent restoration of 4G access for mobile phones, the communications blockade has seriously hampered civic participation, as well as business, livelihoods, education, and access to health-care and medical information. Raids against human rights defenders in October and November exemplify the continued restrictions on civil society, and resulting impact on the rights of the people of Kashmir to impart and receive information, and to engage in free, open debate on Government policies affecting them. Internet access in Pakistan-Administered Kashmir also remains a serious problem, prompting student protests in the past year.

In Pakistan, the unequal status of women continues to result in widespread denial of their rights, from education to the right to make decisions about their own lives; excessive maternal mortality; poverty, and high levels of violence and sexual violence against women and girls. Last year, CEDAW found "persistent discriminatory stereotypes" and expressed concern at the prevalence of child marriage and forced marriage, as well as so-called "honour" based crimes. Women from religious minority communities are particularly vulnerable to forced marriage accompanied by forced conversion. I urge Pakistan to support and protect women human rights defenders and journalists who are at the forefront of efforts to promote legal and societal change.

In China, strong progress has been made over the last year in reducing the prevalence of COVID 19 and its severe impact on the enjoyment of a broad range of human rights. At the same time, fundamental rights and civic freedoms continue to be curtailed in the name of national security and the COVID-19 response. Activists, lawyers and human rights defenders – as well as some foreign nationals – face arbitrary criminal charges, detention or unfair trials. In the Hong Kong Special Administrative Region, more than 600 people are being investigated for participating in various forms of protests – some under the new National Security Law. In the Xinjiang Uyghur Autonomous Region, information that is in the public domain indicates the need for independent and comprehensive assessment of the human rights situation. My Office continues to assess the alleged patterns of human rights violations, including reports of arbitrary detention, ill-treatment and sexual violence in institutions; coercive labour practises; and erosion of social and cultural rights. I am confident that through our ongoing dialogue we will find mutually agreeable parameters for my visit to China.

Madam President,

Across the Americas, the impact of COVID-19 has been heightened by weak social security systems; long-standing structural inequalities and discrimination – especially those experienced by Afro-descendant and indigenous peoples; poorly diversified economies; and high numbers of informal workers. Recent data indicates that a major socio-economic and humanitarian crisis may be looming, with poverty rates that could reach over 37% this year in Latin America and the Caribbean. Overall, the Economic Commission for Latin America and the Caribbean estimates that the region faces a "lost decade", following the worst GDP contraction in the region's history.

In recent years, many countries in the Americas – including Bolivia, Chile, Colombia, Ecuador, Guatemala, Haiti, Honduras, Mexico and Peru – have seen growing movements of social protest. While every situation is distinct, they all broadly focus on inadequate access to economic and social rights; discrimination; impunity; and allegations of corruption. In several countries, demonstrations have been met with the excessive use of force. The pandemic's unfolding socio-economic and humanitarian crisis risks further deepening this discontent, and could trigger a new wave of social unrest. I encourage all States to take measures to prevent further deterioration of the situation, including through guarantees of meaningful and effective participation in the socio-economic pandemic response. I also call for all States to protect the rights to freedom of association and peaceful assembly, and to ensure that demonstrations are managed in compliance with international human rights standards.

In Brazil and other countries of the Amazon and Pantanal regions, reduced enforcement of environmental laws during the pandemic has led to increased illegal mining and illegal logging, with particularly damaging impact on indigenous peoples. Care must be taken to ensure that these territories are better protected from extractive industries and monoculture farming – including in the post-pandemic recovery. Across the region, I am concerned by continued attacks on environmental activists, human rights defenders and journalists, including killings, as well as by the misuse of criminal laws to silence critical voices.

In several States, increasingly tight border controls and the use of security forces to halt migrants are further increasing the risks to people on the move. Last month's discovery of the charred bodies of 19 people – at least 14 of them Guatemalan migrants, together with their alleged smugglers – close to Mexico's border with the U.S. is a stark example. The militarization of border management by Ecuador, Peru and Chile is particularly concerning in the context of the continued unprecedented movement of Venezuelans, with 5.28 million people estimated leaving or remaining outside their country this year. These issues include worrying reports that people are being expelled without due evaluation of their vulnerability or protection needs.

In the United States of America, we welcome broad new measures to tackle structural inequalities and systemic racism. These include executive actions to redress racially discriminatory federal housing policies; combat xenophobia; and reaffirm commitments to tribal sovereignty and the full consultation of indigenous peoples. To adequately address systemic inequalities and injustices, social and economic rights must be placed at the core of the response. We also welcome new steps to end several migration policies that violated the human rights of migrants and refugees, including executive orders to end the family separation policy. I encourage further measures to tackle remaining issues, such as the massive detention of migrants, through the implementation of alternatives to detention.

In Haiti, high levels of insecurity and poverty, as well as controversy over the end-date of the President's mandate are contributing to a disturbing increase in social tensions. Arbitrary detentions have been reported, as well as the excessive use of force to disperse protest, and attacks on human rights defenders and journalists, as well as gang abuses on local populations. The current deadlock risks jeopardizing the rule of law and civic space, and could further destabilize the country. I urge the authorities to guarantee the separation of powers, and call on all parties to address their differences through peaceful means, so as to prevent the recurrence of protracted civil protest and a further increase of violence.

Madam President,

It has been a decade since the Arab uprisings, or "Arab Spring" swept through the Middle East and North Africa – a movement that inspired many with its spontaneity, diversity and call for social justice. The demands by hundreds of thousands of people for Governments to uphold economic and social rights; ensure more equitable sharing of the benefits of development; put an end to repressive policies and corruption; and open the democratic spaces echoed through the streets of countries across the world. And yet, ten years on, many countries in the region continue to suffer very serious inequalities. Repressive policies have, in many cases, been strengthened – and some of the valuable gains made by civic movements are being undermined. Despite these setbacks, I remain optimistic that justice and human rights can be realized across the Middle East and North Africa – and that progress in this direction will ensure deep and lasting progress for development and peace.

The terrible suffering of the people of Syria also marks a grim anniversary. Next month it will be ten years since demonstrations swept through parts of the country. Their violent repression by government forces then escalated into today's deadly military conflict, with regional and international implications. Sporadic violence – including targeted killings, use of improvised explosive devices, and shelling – continues. Severe economic deterioration, exacerbated by the impact of COVID-19, continues to compound the humanitarian crisis. I deeply hope there will be tangible progress by the Constitutional Committee, with the voices and rights of Syrians – including young people and its civil society – at the centre of discussion. It is essential that international actors seek to bridge divides, and put the needs and rights of the Syrian people at the forefront of this process.

I remain concerned about continuing restrictions on freedoms of expression, association, and peaceful assembly in Egypt, including those directed against human rights defenders and other activists. In November last year, three human rights defenders working for the Egyptian Initiative for Personal Rights were arrested and detained pending investigation on terrorism-related charges, publishing false news, and using an internet account to spread false information that undermines public security. While they were released a month later, numerous other human rights defenders, journalists, and activists remain detained, or subjected to asset freezes and travel bans on the basis of vague charges and national security laws.

In Jordan, I am dismayed by increasing restrictions on the rights to freedom of expression – including against journalists reporting on the authorities' response to COVID-19 and its impact on vulnerable groups. The case of the Jordanian Teacher's Syndicate labour union – in which gag orders have been imposed on all news reports or comments – is also troubling. I encourage the Government to engage in dialogue with independent voices, and to view media freedoms, and the promotion of all civic freedoms, as a vital foundation for sound public policies.

In Saudi Arabia, I welcome the release of women's rights campaigner Loujain al-Hathloul, although I regret that others continue to be unjustly detained. I also welcome announced plans to issue new legislation to strengthen human rights guarantees, including with respect to family law and personal status. I urge the authorities to also establish legislative frameworks to uphold the rights to freedom of expression, peaceful assembly and association for everyone in the Kingdom.

In Iraq, targeted killings, threats and intimidation continue against civil society activists, human rights defenders and journalists. The near-total lack of accountability for the violations and abuses committed against demonstrators is a significant obstruction to the development of the public's trust in institutions and the country's future. I note that in October 2020 the Prime Minister ordered the establishment of a fact-finding body; however, it remains unclear whether that body is operational. In the Kurdistan region, activists and protesters have been subjected to arbitrary arrest and detention, with many detainees denied basic due process rights, including access to lawyers.

In Iran, an apparently coordinated campaign has been targeting minority groups since December, including in Sistan and Baluchestan; Khuzestan; and in the Kurdish provinces. Mass arrests and enforced disappearances have been reported, as well as increasing numbers of executions, following deeply flawed processes. Across the country, the exercise of civic freedoms and political or critical expression continue to be targeted through national security laws, criminal prosecution and intimidation. I am concerned at persistent impunity for human rights violations, including violations that occurred in the contexts of protests in 2018 and 2019.

I welcome the formation of a new coalition Government in Yemen, although I regret that it gives no representation to Yemeni women – half the population. The attack on Aden airport on 30 December was particularly shocking. I welcome recent measures by third parties, which strengthen hopes for a negotiated settlement – but these diplomatic moves will not immediately alleviate the widespread malnutrition, forced displacement and attacks on education and health facilities that inflict so much suffering on Yemen's people, together with numerous violations of civil and political rights. I encourage all Member States to make firm commitments at the pledging conference for Yemen on 1 March. I trust the de facto authorities in Sana'a will swiftly issue a visa to my representative.

In Algeria, demonstrations in several provinces continue to mark the anniversary of the Hirak pro-democracy movement. I welcome the decision to hold parliamentary elections early this year, and the release of more than 35 people active in Hirak. I urge the Government to continue on the path of dialogue, and to immediately release all those detained for peaceful participation in demonstrations. There is no doubt that fair and genuine democratic elections which express the will of the people are essential to securing the legitimate authority of governments, and the public trust.

I welcome recent political developments in Libya, and the work we have undertaken with UNSMIL to ensure that human rights are integral to the political agenda and roadmap towards peace. I am also encouraged by the establishment of specialized courts on violence against women and children in Tripoli and Bengazi, and by the fact that five out of the six judges appointed are women. I further commend efforts to revise Libya's law on combating violence against women and girls; this is particularly urgent, given high levels of gender-based violence.

Madam President,

In Ethiopia, it is crucial that full and unimpeded access be immediately given to the whole of the Tigray region, for both humanitarian and human rights workers. Alarming allegations of serious violations committed by all parties during more than three months of conflict include mass killings, extrajudicial executions, and other attacks on civilians, including sexual violence. Credible investigation into all these allegations is vital, with accountability for perpetrators, and my Office stands ready to support. I am also disturbed by reported abductions and forcible returns of Eritrean refugees living in Tigray – some reportedly at the hands of Eritrean forces. At least 15,000 Eritreans who had taken refuge are unaccounted for following the destruction of their shelters. Coupled with growing insecurity in other parts of Ethiopia, the conflict in Tigray could have serious impact on regional stability and human rights. I urge the peaceful resolution of this conflict, and also call for more efforts to resolve the sharply increasing inter-communal violence taking place in other regions of Ethiopia, such as Benishangul-Gumuz and Oromia.

In Uganda, I am concerned that Presidential Directives and other regulations intended to combat COVID-19 have been used to arrest and detain political opponents, journalists and perceived critics of the Government. During the recent electoral process, many opposition supporters were killed and seriously injured, while opposition candidates, human rights defenders and journalists were arbitrarily arrested and detained, ill-treated – and in some instances have disappeared. The stigmatisation of LGBTI individuals, which falsely scapegoats them for the spread of COVID-19, has resulted in arbitrary arrests and detentions, and raids and closures of LGBTI shelters. I call on the authorities to observe human rights standards in all security operations and to promptly and thoroughly investigate all reports of human rights violations.

In Tanzania, efforts to thwart election campaigning by the opposition in the pre-election period included intimidation and violence; arrests of opposition members; and media restrictions, including restricted access to the Internet and social media. Allegations of unlawful killings, arbitrary arrests and illegal detention, and torture were also reported during and after the election, notably in Zanzibar. Transparent investigation of all these allegations is essential. I am also concerned by apparent official attempts to deny the reality of COVID-19 in the country – including measures to criminalise recognition of the pandemic and related information.

This could have serious impact on Tanzanians' right to health. I note reports of pushbacks of hundreds of asylum-seekers from Mozambique and the DRC, as well as continued reports of torture, enforced disappearances and forced returns of Burundian refugees.

In Mali, I encourage swift action by the transitional authorities to ensure prosecution of the suspected perpetrators of serious human rights violations, including among the security forces. The International Commission of Inquiry on Mali has issued important recommendations, and I look forward to their implementation by relevant States and key actors, in order to advance the cause of accountability and combat impunity. I also encourage immediate steps to enhance civilian participation and leadership in the political space, with specific focus on the equality of women and their participation in administrative and legislative bodies. I am particularly concerned by last year's increase in killings and other serious violations and abuses, as well as the sharply reduced democratic space.

In Malawi, mob-justice attacks have more than tripled over the past year, according to official police statistics. They appear to include an increasing number of attacks against older women accused of practicing witchcraft, as well as against people with albinism. Attempted abductions of children with albinism have also been reported, and are presumed linked to a market for body parts, to be used in rituals. I am also troubled by the significant rise in sexual violence against women and girls recorded in Malawi after schools were temporarily closed last year, as well as a 400% increase in child marriage, and teenage pregnancy, in some districts of the country. Fear of the pandemic and increasing poverty may be factors in this increased violence, which calls for a stronger and more accountable police force, as well as stronger protection measures.

In Somalia, I am increasingly concerned about repeated attempts to dismantle the already weak legal protection afforded to children and to women, including with respect to sexual violence and child marriage. I reiterate the need for the 2018 Sexual Offenses Bill to be adopted without delay in the form approved by Cabinet.

In Sudan, I welcome the Joint Council's approval of ratification of the Convention Against Torture and the Convention for the Protection of All Persons from Enforced Disappearance. In the Darfur region, incidents of intercommunal violence and other major protection concerns persist. I acknowledge important recent actions by the Government to contain the violence, but I also urge prompt measures to ensure accountability for the grave human rights violations of the past, including remedy for victims. Such efforts are especially important given their deterrent impact. The continued reoccurrence of violence in Darfur points to core grievances, making the full application of the Government's reform agenda a matter of urgency. Our Office is providing technical assistance to several major institutional reform efforts, and I will continue to encourage international development partners to prioritise support for reforms.

In Guinea, while I welcome the authorities' cooperation with my Office in country, the arrest and detention of opposition members and civil society activists on spurious charges of undermining the internal security of the State, in the context of last year's presidential elections, severely undermines the foundations of democratic governance. I call on the Government to release all those detained for exercising their rights to freedom of expression, peaceful assembly and participation, and to ensure fair trials for those charged with criminal offences. I also call on the authorities to expedite the trials of the common law detainees and to improve their food and health conditions. In the context of COVID-19, I reiterate my call for the release of those particularly vulnerable, including older detainees and those who are sick, as well as low-risk offenders.

I remain concerned about the situation in Comoros, including the crackdown on democratic space, with continued restrictions on freedoms of expression and of the press; continued and often lengthy detention of civil society activists and members of the political opposition; and unjustified prosecutions of journalists. I call on the Government to maintain the civic space and uphold human rights and fundamental freedoms.

Madam President,

Protecting civic space and the right of all people to participate are threshold rights: they open up further impacts that build resilience, prosperity and peace.

Today, in every region of the world, people are being left behind – or pushed even further behind – as the coronavirus pandemic continues to gather pace. They are being excluded, not only from development, and from opportunities, but from participation in the decisions that profoundly shape their lives and futures.

This makes us all weaker. It heightens grievances that are destabilizing. It means we miss perspectives and expertise that could inform and strengthen our initiatives. It shields corruption and abuses, by silencing feedback. This is why my Office, this Council and all other stakeholders – in the UN family, in regional organisations and around the world – must speak out against measures that silence civil society. Because working to

> defend our rights – and standing up to support human rights defenders – is vital to humanity's future.

Updates by the High Commissioner are calls to conscience. In a few instances, the Human Rights Council is moved to act. Often, it is not!!! Politics trump principle. The Council's inaction on the foregoing situations of concern presented to it by the High Commissioner are a damning indictment of itself.

5 Protection Activities of Special Procedures of the Council

At the request of the Human Rights Council, the Secretary-General presents to it each year a report on Conclusions and recommendations of special procedures. This is an informative document, and the report submitted on 22 December, 2020,[2] covering activities for the preceding year records that over the three sessions of the Council in 2020, 64 country reports were presented by thematic mandate holders: 10 reports concerned States in Africa; 21 reports concerned States in the Asia-Pacific region; 9 reports related to Eastern Europe; 11 reports related to Latin America and the Caribbean; 13 reports related to States in the Group of Western European and other States.

In addition, the following country-specific mandate holders submitted reports: the Special Rapporteur on the situation of human rights in Belarus; the Special Rapporteur on the situation of human rights in Cambodia; the Independent Expert on the situation of human rights in the Central African Republic; the Special Rapporteur on the situation of human rights in the Democratic People's Republic of Korea; the Special Rapporteur on the situation of human rights in Eritrea; the Special Rapporteur on the situation of human rights in the Islamic Republic of Iran; the Independent Expert on the situation of human rights in Mali; the Special Rapporteur on the situation of human rights in Myanmar; the Independent Expert on the situation of human rights in Somalia; and the Independent Expert on the situation of human rights in the Sudan.[3]

---

2 A/HRC/46/24, 22 December, 2020.

3 A/HRC/46/24, paras. 75-81.

6 Conclusion

At its founding in 1945 the United Nations committed itself to working for peace and development on the foundations of universal respect for human rights. The Charter and the Universal Declaration of Human Rights provided the human rights components of the contemporary international constitutional order, which have subsequently been expanded by documents such as the United Nations Millennium Declaration. Article 68 of the Charter provided for the establishment of a Commission on Human Rights which functioned between 19476 and 2005 and which has since been replaced by the Human Rights Council.

The Commission on Human Rights undoubtedly made great contributions to the advancement of human rights universally. It is the Commission which launched the vision of an International Bill of Human Rights consisting of the Universal Declaration, the two International Covenants, and Measures of Implementation. The Commission developed the Special Procedures, whose mission is to examine issues and situations of gross violations of human rights. But the Commission was always an imperfect, political body with a human rights mission. There were many occasions when, for political reasons, it failed to act for the principled protection of human rights – even if it did do so in respect of other situations. In the end, voices were raised, calling for its replacement and these succeeded in 2006 with its replacement by the Human Rights Council.

Almost from the outset, the Human Rights Council itself has come in for heavy criticism on three main grounds: first that, for political reasons, it fails to take principled action in respect of many situations of gross violations of human rights; second, that its membership seeks to weaken the special procedures, the mandate holders examining issues or situations of gross violations of human rights; and third, that it has over-concentrated on alleged gross violations committee by Israeli occupation forces in Palestine while refusing to take similar action in respect of other equally serious or, at time, even more serious situations.

The first criticism is a valid one. Its predecessor, while suffering from similar blemishes as the Council, had been more willing to discuss country situations and to adopt strong resolutions on them – even if it also was selective on many occasions. Like the Commission, however, the Council is a political body, and whether it will ever be free of political machinations is doubtful. But then there is a fundamental policy issue: does the United Nations not need a political human rights body? Many would answer this question in the affirmative and, while criticizing its shortcomings, would look to other institutions such as the treaty monitoring bodies and the UN High Commissioner for Human Rights to compensate for its weaknesses.

The second criticism also has a fair measure of justification. While the Council did maintain the system of special procedures and has declared its commitment to their objective functioning, its membership keeps the mandate holders under scrutiny and pressure – especially when they act vigorously for the protection of human rights. Members of the Council would prefer more dialogue with offending governments rather than outright condemnation. Mandate-holders have come in for targeted attacks from governments accused, and from their supporters. If this trend continues it would call into question the validity of the Council.

The third criticism has two parts: it is very much the case that Israel has come in for far more criticism than any other Member State. This is wrong: every government that violates human rights should come in for criticism from the Council. Other governments guilty of gross violations should also be condemned and Israel should not be singled out. The second aspect concerns the degree of criticism of Israel for its actions in Palestine. Views may vary on this and the issue is open to discussion. In the midst of conflict, prolonged occupation, expanding settlements, and suicide bombings, the human rights situation in Palestine is a wrenching one and the need for a political settlement is acute. Hopefully, when a political settlement is eventually reached this criticism will be lifted from the Council.

So, the Council has an important human rights mandate; it is a political body with many imperfections; but there is need for a high-level political organ in the United Nations dealing with human rights; and, in the nature of things, a political body, even one dealing with human rights, will be marked by the interests and attitudes of its members. Having said this, the question still deserves to be posed: has the Council, notwithstanding its imperfections, been putting building blocks for protection that might be useful in the future? The General Assembly and the Security Council are both highly political bodies. Nevertheless, from early on in their existence, repertories have been published in the hope of documenting and systematizing their practice and in the hope of reminding them of their stances in the past so as to help them maintain some measure of consistency in their policies and responses to situations. There is need for a similar repertory of the practice of the Human Rights Council on its protection approaches. This is one of the aims of this book.

CHAPTER 4

Prevention

1 Introduction

The Council's mandate as set out in paragraph 5(f) of General Assembly resolution 60/251 includes contributing, through dialogue and cooperation, towards the prevention of human rights violations and responding promptl6y to human rights emergencies. The Council has organized a number of discussions, and requested several reports, on the implementation of its prevention mandate. The NGO Universal Rights Group has been particularly active on this issue and has organized meetings with the Council's membership, and prepared studies on the topic. However, because of the political stances within its membership, the Council has not yet worked out tangible ways of implementing its prevention mandate beyond some general pronouncements and a few resolutions on preventive strategies in particular areas.

By way of general pronouncements, the Council considers that prevention, to be effective, requires long-term engagement and a forward-looking approach in identifying and addressing the risk factors and root causes of crises which, if not tackled, may lead to human rights emergencies and conflicts.

In the Council's assessment, the bulk of preventive work takes place at the national level, on the initiative and under the direction of national authorities, through the implementation of the State's international human rights obligations and commitments, *inter alia* through the work of national mechanisms for implementation, reporting and follow-up.

The Council has acknowledged the important role played by national human rights institutions, civil society organizations and human rights defenders in preventing human rights violations, including by providing information on early warning signs and on patterns of human rights violations.

The existing mechanisms of the Council, particularly the universal periodic review, the special procedures, the complaints procedure, the Advisory Committee and the open-ended intergovernmental working groups contribute to the prevention of human rights violations and to the promotion and protection of human rights.

The Council has encouraged all its mechanisms to integrate prevention into their work and, where appropriate, into their reporting, in accordance with their respective mandates. It has encouraged States and all other relevant

 | DOI:10.1163/9789004504950_006

stakeholders to consider the recommendations on prevention made in the report of the rapporteurs.[1]

The Council has requested the United Nations High Commissioner for Human Rights to continue to strengthen the capability of the Office of the High Commissioner to identify, verify, manage and analyse data and early warning signs emanating from all sources, including from States, human rights mechanisms, national human rights institutions, civil society organizations, human rights defenders, United Nations country teams and the Office's field presences, and to address them in accordance with the High Commissioner's mandate.

The Council has also called upon the High Commissioner, where the Office of the High Commissioner identifies patterns of human rights violations that point to a heightened risk of a human rights emergency, to continue to bring that information to the attention of the members and observers of the Human Rights Council in a manner that reflects the urgency of the situation and that maintains space for dialogue and cooperation with the State and region concerned, including through briefings.

The Council has signalled its readiness to resort, on a case-by-case basis and where appropriate, to work formats that enhance dialogue and cooperation with the State and region concerned, with the aim of addressing the root causes of, and preventing, further human rights violations and responding promptly to human rights emergencies.

The Council has requested the Secretary-General to bring regularly to the attention of the relevant bodies of the United Nations the reports of the Human Rights Council relevant to prevention. It has also invited the Chair of the UN Peacebuilding Commission to brief it on an annual basis on the work of the Commission, including in relation to country situations that are on the Council's agenda.[2]

2 Pronouncements of the Council on Prevention in Thematic Areas

We refer below to some resolutions of the Council in which it has highlighted the role of prevention on some thematic issues.

1 See A/HRC/46/24.

2 HRC resolution 45/31 of 7 October, 2020.: The contribution of the Human Rights Council to the prevention of human rights violations. Adopted on a recorded vote of 32 to 3 with 11 abstentions. Countries voting against included Venezuela. Among the abstainers were India, Indonesia, Nigeria, Pakistan and Philippines.

Prevention of Genocide: In resolution 7/25, on the prevention of genocide, adopted without a vote, the Council reaffirmed the significance of the Convention on the Prevention and Punishment of the Crime of Genocide as an effective international instrument for the prevention and punishment of the crime of genocide and reiterated the responsibility of each individual State to protect its population from genocide, which entails the prevention of such a crime, including incitement to it, through appropriate and necessary means.[3]

Combatting Impunity as a Preventive Strategy: In resolution No. 9 adopted at its ninth session, on the protection of the human rights of civilians in armed conflict, the Council, called upon all States to respect the human rights of civilians in armed conflicts and stressed the importance of combating impunity in order to prevent violations of international human rights law and international humanitarian law against civilians in armed conflicts, and urged States, in accordance with their international obligations, to bring perpetrators of such crimes to justice.

Preventable maternal mortality and morbidity: In its resolution 11/8, the Council has recognized that most instances of maternal mortality and morbidity are preventable and that preventable maternal mortality and morbidity is a health, development and human rights challenge that also requires the effective promotion and protection of the human rights of women and girls, in particular their right to life, to be equal in dignity, to education, to be free to seek, receive and impart information, to enjoy the benefits of scientific progress, to freedom from discrimination, and to enjoy the highest attainable standard of physical and mental health, including sexual and reproductive health.

Trafficking: The Council has affirmed that it is essential to place the protection of human rights at the centre of measures taken to prevent and end trafficking in persons, and to protect, assist and provide access to adequate redress to victims, including the possibility of obtaining compensation from the perpetrators.

3 Preventive Actions of Special Procedures of the Council

At the request of the Human Rights Council, the Secretary-General presents to it each year a report on Conclusions and recommendations of special procedures. This is an informative document, and the report submitted on 22

3 Resolution 7/25, adopted without a vote on 28 March, 2008.

December, 2020,[4] covering activities for the preceding year itemises the following preventive activities of the special procedures:

> "26. Mandate holders continued to focus on the prevention of human rights violations and on peace and security issues.
>
> "27. The Special Rapporteur on the promotion of truth, justice, reparation and guarantees on non-recurrence highlighted the need for active and multidimensional memory policies to respond adequately to past crimes and prevent their recurrence (A/HRC/45/45).
>
> "28. The Special Rapporteur on the promotion and protection of human rights and fundamental freedoms while countering terrorism focused on the human rights impact of policies and practices aimed at preventing and countering violent extremism (A/HRC/43/46).
>
> "29. The Independent Expert on the enjoyment of human rights by persons with albinism considered prevention measures to ensure the protection of persons with albinism worldwide (A/75/170).
>
> "30. The Working Group on Arbitrary Detention addressed the issue of prevention of arbitrary detention of liberty in the context of public health emergencies (A/HRC/45/16).
>
> "31. The Working Group on the issue of human rights and transnational corporations and other business enterprises focused on business-related human rights abuse in conflict and post-conflict contexts (A/75/212).
>
> "32. The Special Rapporteur on the situation of human rights defenders analysed the situation of human rights defenders operating in conflict and post-conflict areas (A/HRC/43/51).
>
> "33. The Working Group on the use of mercenaries as a means of violating human rights and impeding the exercise of the right of peoples to self-determination examined the evolution of the use of mercenaries and related actors in the light of the changes in the nature of contemporary armed conflicts (A/75/259).
>
> "34. The Special Rapporteur on extra-judicial, summary or arbitrary executions examined in her report (A/HRC/44/38) how drone attacks pose a fundamental challenge to international legal standards and the institutions established to safeguard peace and security.
>
> ...
>
> "86. The issue of prevention of human rights violations was addressed by the Working Group on Enforced or Involuntary Disappearances in its

4 A/HRC/46/24, 22 December, 2020.

> reports on Tajikistan (A/HRC/45/13/Add.1) and Kyrgyzstan (A/HRC/45/13/Add.2); the Working Group on Arbitrary Detention in its report on Qatar (A/HRC/45/16/Add.2); the Special Rapporteur on the promotion of truth, justice, reparation and guarantees of non-recurrence in his reports on Sri Lanka (A/HRC/45/Add.1) and the Gambia (A/HRC/45/45/Add.3); the Special Rapporteur on the human rights of internally displaced persons in her report on Iraq (A/HRC/44/41/Add.1); and the Special Rapporteur on torture and other cruel, inhuman or degrading treatment or punishment in his report on the Comoros (A/HRC/43/49/Add.1).

The foregoing instances show the special procedures mandate holders of the Council engaged in concrete efforts to help prevent the commission of gross violations of human rights.

4 Early Warning from the UN High Commissioner

The High Commissioner for Human Rights sometimes draws the attention of the Council to situations of concern. Thus, in a report that she presented to the Human Rights Council on 9 February, 2021, submitted at the request of the Council, UN High Commissioner Michelle Bachelet stated: "..the United Nations High Commissioner for Human Rights is deeply concerned by the trends that have emerged over the past year, which may represent early warning signs of a deteriorating human rights situation."[5] In her report, the High Commissioner highlighted that developments over the past year had fundamentally changed the environment for advancing reconciliation, accountability and human rights in Sri Lanka, eroded democratic checks and balances and the civic space, and permitted the resurfacing of a dangerous exclusionary and majoritarian discourse. Those trends threatened to reverse the limited but important gains that had been made in recent years and risked leading to a return to the policies and practices that had given rise to the grave violations of the past. The High Commissioner believed that the Human Rights Council should urgently pay attention to these early warning signs and continue its close monitoring of, and engagement on, developments in Sri Lanka. She urged Member States to pursue alternative international options for ensuring justice and reparations and to strengthen capacity to make progress.[6]

---

5 A/HRC/46/20, Summary.

6 Idem. See also, Idem, para. 2.

Specifically, the High Commissioner reported to the Council:

> Significant challenges and negative trends that have emerged over the past year have profoundly changed the environment for reconciliation, accountability and human rights, as well as the achievement of the 2030 Agenda for Sustainable Development. Despite some of the successful efforts made by the Government to contain the COVID-19 pandemic, its social and economic impact has been deep and exacerbated social disparities.[7]

The High Commissioner continued:

> The High Commissioner … is deeply concerned about the increased use of ethno-nationalistic and majoritarian rhetoric and symbols by the President and other senior government figures and about the fact that pubic policies appear to exclusively reflect the perceived interests of the Sinhala Buddhist majority and show minimal consideration for minority communities. Ethnic and religious minority communities are left behind and excluded in such official discourse and are often perceived and treated as posing a threat. Such an approach has serious negative implications for reconciliation, peacebuilding and religious tolerance and carries the seeds of future violence and conflict.[8]
>
> Furthermore, "The High Commissioner is concerned that the Government has continued to use the Prevention of Terrorism Act despite repeated calls over many years by United Nations human rights mechanisms to repeal it. …
>
> The High Commissioner is also concerned by a recent series of deaths in policy custody and in the context of police encounters with alleged criminal gangs. …
>
> These incidents reflect the persistence of long-standing and endemic patterns of custodial deaths, torture and other ill-treatment, and extrajudicial killings by law enforcement officials with impunity. Furthermore, OHCHR has continued to receive credible allegations, through well-known human rights organizations, of abductions, torture and sexual violence by Sri Lankan security forces since the adoption of Human Rights

7 Idem, para. 18.

8 Idem, para.29.

> Council resolution 30/1, including during the past year, which need to be credibly investigated.[9]

The High Commissioner concluded her report as follows:

> Nearly 12 years since the end of the war, domestic initiatives for accountability and reconciliation have repeatedly failed to produce results, more deeply entrenching impunity and exacerbating victims' distrust of the system …
>
> ..[T]he High Commissioner is deeply concerned by the trends that have emerged during the past year, which represent clear early warning signs of a deteriorating human rights situation and a significantly heightened risk of future violations, and therefore calls for strong preventive action.[10]

The High Commissioner recommended to the Human Rights Council and Member States of the UN to: request OHCHR to enhance its monitoring of the human rights situation in Sri Lanka, including progress towards accountability and reconciliation, and report regularly to the Council; and to support a dedicated capacity to collect and preserve evidence and other related information for future accountability processes, to advocate for victims and survivors and to support relevant judicial proceedings in member States with competent jurisdiction.[11]

In presenting her report to the Human Rights Council on 24 February, 2021, High Commissioner Michelle Bachelet made the following eloquent plea for action by the Human Rights Council:

> This is a key juncture for the Council's engagement with Sri Lanka. As my report indicates, nearly 12 years after the end of the armed conflict, domestic initiatives have repeatedly failed to ensure justice for victims and promote reconciliation. Despite commitments made in 2015, the current Government, like its predecessor, has failed to pursue genuine truth-seeking or accountability processes.
>
> The impact on thousands of survivors, from all communities, is devastating. Moreover, the systems, structure, policies and personnel that gave

9 Idem, paras. 36-39.
10 Idem, paras. 52-53.
11 Idem, paras. 61 (a) and (b).

rise to such grave violations in the past remain – and have recently been reinforced.

Addressing grievances and redressing past violations are critical prevention tools at the core of the Council's work. Our report highlights disturbing trends over the past year, which warn of a serious deterioration in key areas.

The space for civil society and independent media, which had grown significantly, is now rapidly shrinking.

The independence of the judiciary, the Human Rights Commission of Sri Lanka, the National Police Commission and other key bodies has been deeply eroded by the recently adopted 20th Constitutional Amendment.

The growing militarisation of key civilian functions is encroaching on democratic governance. The continued failure to implement comprehensive reforms – or to vet personnel – leaves in place security and military officers who have been implicated in alleged grave crimes and violations.

Tamil and Muslim minorities are being excluded by divisive and discriminatory rhetoric including from the highest State officials.

The policy of forced cremation of COVID-19 victims has caused pain and distress to the minority Muslim and Christian communities.

In other words, long-standing structural and systemic issues persist in Sri Lanka, and now there are clear warning signs that past patterns of violations could be repeated.

Successive Government commissions have failed to credibly establish truth and ensure accountability. Indeed, the Government has obstructed investigations and judicial proceedings into emblematic human rights cases.

The latest commission of inquiry, appointed in January 2021 to review the findings of previous commissions, promises to repeat this cycle without meaningful result.

By repeatedly failing to advance accountability for past human rights violations committed, and by withdrawing its support for the Council's resolution 30/1 and related measures, the Government has largely closed the door on the possibility of genuine progress to end impunity through a national process.

For these reasons, I call on the Council to explore new ways to advance various types of accountability at the international level, for all parties, and seek redress for victims, including by supporting a dedicated capacity to collect and preserve evidence and information for future accountability processes, as well as to support relevant judicial proceedings in Member States.

> My Office stands ready to continue monitoring the human rights situation, including progress towards accountability and reconciliation.[12]

How did the Human Rights Council deal with this powerful presentation by the High Commissioner? The short press releases issued by the UN reported that in the discussion on Sri Lanka, some speakers welcomed the detailed report and its focus on the issue of accountability for past violations, as well as the current human rights situation. They said that the militarisation of the current government and its impact on the Tamil and Muslim communities was a cause for concern. They thought that the shrinking space for civil society was of particular concern, and they urged Sri Lanka to review the Prevention of Terrorism Act. They regretted that nearly a decade of Council engagement had not led to accountability for past war crimes, as alleged perpetrators had been appointed to senior government positions, facilitating further abuses.

Other speakers, however said that the report lacked contextual analysis, did not take into account the effects of the COVID-19 pandemic and Sri Lanka's comments, and, so they asserted, mischaracterised Sri Lanka's long history of fighting terrorism, as well as its successful cooperation with the Universal Periodic Review. They welcomed Sri Lanka's efforts to improve the human rights situation and its openness in discussing its issues.

Commenting on the discussion, the Deputy High Commissioner, in her concluding remarks, noted that OHCHR enjoyed a very frank and open relationship with the Government of Sri Lanka. Victims had a central place in the design of accountability mechanisms, and the Office provided support in this regard. She added that legislative reforms must comply with international obligations.[13]

The resolution that the Human Rights Council eventually adopted on the situation in Sri Lanka did not rise to the occasion and focused, instead, on technical assistance to the Government of Sri Lanka.

---

12 UN Press Release, "46th session of the Human Rights Council. Report of OHCHR on promoting reconciliation, accountability and human rights in Sri Lanka (A/HRC/46/20) – Statement by Michelle Bachelet, UN High Commissioner for Human Rights, 24 February, 2021.

13 See UN Press Release, Human Rights Council Concludes Interactive Dialogue on Sri Lanka. …

5 Tackling Root Causes of Violations

Various activities take place under the auspices of the Human Rights Council with the aim of addressing the root causes of gross violations of human rights. On 25 February, 2021, for example, the Special Rapporteur on freedom of religion or belief submitted to the Council a report on Countering Islamophobia/Anti-Muslim Hatred to Eliminate Discrimination and Intolerance Based on Religion or Belief.[14]

The Special Rapporteur, Mr Ahmed Shaheed expressed his deep alarm at the frequent, widespread nature of violence targeting Muslims worldwide, including incidents where authorities allegedly had incited, engaged in or failed to respond to violence. He recalled studies identifying a dialectic between State policies and practices that discriminated against Muslims and the Islamophobia that fuelled individual assailants to carry out violent attacks against Muslims and their property. He stated: "When the religious practices, beliefs, employment, education and immigration statuses of Muslims are repressed by States, or when State actors advance stigmatizing discourses against Muslims, private citizens can be emboldened to attack Muslims, and may even consider themselves to be acting in defence of their nation-state or their culture. Rather than being 'isolated incidents' they argue, street-level hate crimes against Muslims are a reproduction of the prejudice stoked by States."[15]

The Special Rapporteur advanced a number of recommendations to States, employers, digital technology companies, the media, civil society, including faith-based actors, and the UN system. These recommendations included the following:

States should repeal all restrictions on the absolute freedom of belief and repeal discriminatory restrictions on the right to manifest one's religion or belief.

States should take all measures necessary to combat direct and indirect forms of discrimination against Muslims.

States should fulfil their obligations to prohibit any advocacy of religious hatred that constitutes incitement to discrimination, hostility or violence.

States should counter discrimination by law enforcement agencies, including by eliminating discriminatory profiling of Muslims and by promoting fair policing.

---

14 A/HRC/46/30.

15 Ibid., para. 44.

States should provide resources to Muslim communities to invest in educational, mentorship and leadership programmes that can build resilience, skills and support socially disadvantaged individuals.

States should collect disaggregated data on hate crime and discrimination against actual or perceived Muslims, including the percentage of investigations and prosecutions undertaken following such complaints and their outcome.

States should ensure the existence of accessible and confidential mechanisms where victims can report incidents of Islamophobic hate crimes and discrimination. Where such mechanism exist, States should ensure that they are easily accessible and function under a victim-based human rights approach, including within the criminal justice system.

States should advise political parties to adopt and enforce ethical guidelines for their representatives' conduct, especially regarding public speech. Party leaders must promptly, clearly and consistently reject expressions of Islamophobic discourse within their parties and in public discourse.

States should address Islamophobic discourse by providing anti-stereotyping training to State officials and educators, removing Islamophobic rhetoric from educational curricula and include content on religious and cultural diversity in their school curricula.

Employers should adopt and implement policies to prevent discrimination within the workplace, including on the basis of religion or belief.

Digital technology companies should ensure community guidelines and terms of use are clear and predictable in their application.

Digital technology companies should increase transparency with regard to their efforts to tackle incitement and hate speech.

The media should adopt guidelines for reporting on Muslims and Islam.

Civil society should promote interfaith engagement, refrain from engaging in incitement to discrimination, hostility and violence against persons based on religion or belief, respect diversity and build solidarity.[16]

These are, without a doubt, complex issues, requiring steady effort over time. But we can here see a Special Rapporteur of the Council sensitizing the world body to the issue of Islamophobia and making practical recommendations for reducing and hopefully preventing Islamophobic practices in the future. Prevention here seeks to address the root causes of gross violations.

16 Ibid, paras.79-95.

6 Conclusion

There is partial protection activity within the Council, especially on the part of its special procedures mandate holders, the High Commissioner for Human Rights, the Council's commissions of inquiry and other similar bodies. But two things stand out: first, depending on the political alignments within the Council, sometimes the Council is forthright in denouncing gross violations and on other occasions it favours 'dialogue and cooperation'. The Council is thus an uneven actor when it comes to the issue of protection. Second, NGOs and civil society representatives often plead to the Council for justice for the victims of gross violations of human rights. Unfortunately, their calls often fall on deaf airs on the part of the Council. Politics, not justice, rules when it comes to the protection role of the Human Rights Council.

The prevention of gross violations of human rights is no easy matter. The responsibility, in the first place is on each government within its own country. Therein lies a structural problem. Numerous governments of the world are lacking in legitimacy or probity and often are themselves the sources of gross violations of human rights. The power of the international community to take preventive actions against such governments is mostly lacking in practice.

Where governments are acting in good faith, and where national human rights institutions exist, they can play a role in studying situations that could boil over and in recommending preventive measures to their respective government, or possibly even to regional and international organizations. Some national human rights institutions do this, but even they face numerous pressures inside countries.

Regional human rights bodies, to the extent that they undertake regular visits to, or dialogues with, their participating countries, may be able to play a preventive role. But it has to be recognized that because the scale of gross violations in the world is so extensive and so massive their success rate is not very high.

The UN Security Council focuses mostly on threats to international peace and security and plays, if at all, only a limited preventive role in the human rights field. Nor does the UN General Assembly. The General Assembly, in its resolution establishing the Human Rights Council, has mandated the Council to contribute, through dialogue and cooperation, towards the prevention of human rights violations and to respond promptly to human rights emergencies.[17]

---

17 G.A. resolution 60/251, para. 5(f).

It would be fair to say that the Human Rights Council, so far, has mainly skirted around this mandate. It has occasionally discussed the issue, mandated brain-storming exercises, and adopted the occasional resolution. But, because of the political complexion of its membership the Council is facing a challenge when it comes to the protection of human rights and that same challenge hobbles it when it comes to the prevention of gross violations of human rights. Alerts are provided by the High Commissioner for Human Rights and by Special Procedures mandate holders, and sometimes the Council acts on such alerts. But then, often, it does not.

So far, because of the political control by the members of the Council, neither the President nor the Bureau has yet undertaken a prevention role. It should be possible for the principal human rights body of the United Nations to mandate its Bureau or its President to play a preventive role while it is not in session and to help it sift through urgent situations and to make recommendations to the Council for consideration when it is in session.

It may be worthwhile, in the future, to explore further possible preventive roles for the President and/or the Bureau of the Council.

CHAPTER 5

Urgent Action

1 Introduction

The Human Rights Council's response to urgent situations calling for a protection response is a an unsatisfactory one. Some urgent action within the framework of the Council is undertaken by special procedures mandate holders, through the convening of special sessions, in limited actions of the President, in actions of the High Commissioner undertaken at the request of the Council, and through its Special Procedures' urgent communications to Governments. The bottom line is that in numerous situations where people are being severely persecuted there is little or no immediate response by the Council. This is a structural defect in the Council that needs to be remedied, dare we say, *urgently*.

The Human Rights Council inherited from its predecessor, and has continued and expanded, a system of 'special procedures': investigators and analysts mandated to act for the protection of human rights. In 2020, special procedure mandate holders presented 134 reports to the Council and 48 reports to the General Assembly.[1] Special procedures mandate holders regularly present to the Council reports on urgent action representations made to Governments.[2]

The website of the Office of High Commissioner for Human Rights carries a document, "Communications sent report", consulted on 27 February, 2021, which shows that in 2020 special procedures mandate holders had sent 368 urgent communications to Governments. In the chapter on Good Offices below we provide a sample selection from this report taken from the months of June and November, 2020.

It is not straightforward to assess the results of such urgent actions by special procedures mandate holders. Governments often simply deny the allegations in question, or provide alleged grounds for the treatment of the persons concerned. The hope of the special procedures mandate holders is that transmitting the information would put Governments on notice that their actions are being monitored by the international community. It would also be hoped that Governments might stop or reduce the violations. In some instances,

1 See UN doc. A/HRC/46/24: Conclusions and recommendations of special procedures: Report of the Secretary-General.

2 Ibid, para. 89.

 | DOI:10.1163/9789004504950_007

Governments of good faith might act to release a detainee or otherwise provide humanitarian relief. This is the nature of the human rights endeavour: one does what is possible in the circumstances to help people undergoing violations, or at risk of them.

On 12 August, 2020, the Special Rapporteur on torture and other cruel, inhuman or degrading treatment of punishment, Nils Melzer, undertook a round of State consultations by questionnaire, inviting all States Members of the United Nations to outline their current procedures for the processing of official communications and country visits transmitted by the Special Rapporteur; to evaluate the effectiveness of their current cooperation with the mandate regarding official communications and country visit requests; and to make recommendations and requests with a view to improving their current cooperation and dialogue with the mandate holder. Of the 195 Governments contacted by the Special Rapporteur, 31 (16 per cent) provided a response.

On 22 January, 2021, the Special Rapporteur submitted a penetrating report analysing the reactions of Governments to urgent actions that he had undertaken during the first four years of his mandate.[3] Between 1 November 2016 and 31 October 2020, the Special Rapporteur had transmitted 514 official communications relating to allegations of torture and ill-treatment to Member States, both individually and jointly with other mandate holders. During the same period, the Special Rapporteur also sent 16 communications to non-State actors.

The Special Rapporteur made a statistical analysis of the communications sent to Governments which showed that in response to 512 communications transmitted by the Special Rapporteur, 186 communications (36 per cent) did not receive any response (no-cooperation); 278 responses (54 per cent) were unsatisfactory (partial cooperation); and 48 responses (10 per cent) were satisfactory (full cooperation). The Special Rapporteur commented: "The low degree of responsiveness and cooperation reflected in the statistics is by no means a recent phenomenon, but has rather been a constant pattern since the establishment of the mandate by the Commission on Human Rights in 1985. In the very first report of the mandate submitted to the Commission (E/CN.4/1986/15), the Special Rapporteur stressed that, while he had transmitted allegations of torture to 33 Governments, only 11 had responded to his requests for information. The comprehensive observation reports prepared by other previous mandate holders reflect similar proportions in terms of both responsiveness and cooperation."[4]

---

3 A/HRC/46/26.

4 Ibid, paras 54-57.

The Special Rapporteur reported that "Most alarmingly, some official statements or communications transmitted ... by the Special Rapporteur have received aggressive responses. The States concerned not only rejected the allegations of human rights violations, but also accused the relevant mandate holders of 'bias', 'inflammatory remarks', 'political motivation', 'violations of the Charter of the United Nations', or 'interference with national sovereignty.' "[5]

He added that "[A] very widespread pattern of 'partial cooperation' with the mandate holder involves unsubstantiated denial, whereby Governments reject or dismiss allegations relating to an act or risk of torture or ill-treatment without providing credible evidence, explanations or counterarguments."[6] Another very common pattern of partial cooperation with the mandate holder involved "obstructive formalism, whereby Governments decline to provide the requested information or to take the recommended protective or corrective measures on the basis of claims of national security, secrecy, policy or constitutional order, or on other excessively formalistic arguments."[7]

Furthermore, "Some States that are frequently solicited by the Special Rapporteur through official communications make significant efforts to give the impression of exemplary cooperation while at the same time *de facto* maintaining a system of institutionalized torture and ill-treatment."[8] The Special Rapporteur concluded his report as follows:

> The vast majority of States' responses to official communications transmitted by the Special Rapporteur on specific allegations of torture or ill-treatment fall short of the standard of 'full cooperation' set by the Human Rights Council, and fail to include the measures of prevention, investigation, prosecution and redress recommended by the Special Rapporteur and legally required under the absolute and non-derogable prohibition of torture and ill-treatment.[9]

This is the world in which the Human Rights Council and its mandate-holders are called upon to operate. The tangible protection of human rights is indeed a difficult task.

5 Ibid, para. 66.
6 Ibid, para. 68.
7 Ibid, para. 70.
8 Ibid, para. 72.
9 Ibid, para. 68.

2 Special Sessions of the Council

The Council's mandate enables it to hold special sessions in situations of human rights emergencies, and the Council has held several such sessions. It has been praised for some of these special sessions and criticized for others on the grounds of alleged bias. We look below at a recent special session of the Council, on the situation of human rights in Myanmar.

Human rights issues in Myanmar, formerly known as Burma, have been on the agenda of the Human Rights Council and its predecessor for decades. UN human rights investigators have looked closely at different aspects of the situation. These have included envoys sent to the country under petitions procedures, special rapporteurs, and commissions of inquiry. A case brought by the Gambia against Myanmar for alleged genocide against the Rohingya population, nearly a million of whom have been expelled from or have fled the country, is, at the time of writing, engaging the attention of the International Court of Justice.

The Human Rights Council was brought into special session on 12 February, 2021 following a military take-over of the country on 1 February 2021. The military take over flew in the face of the results of widely recognized democratic elections that had returned the party of Daw Aung San Suu Kyi overwhelmingly to office. The coup took place on the eve of, and prevented the swearing in of, the new parliament and the new government. In making the request for a special session, the delegation of the United Kingdom, on behalf of some fifty requesting Member and Observer States stated: "A special session is needed because of the importance and urgency of the situation."

Addressing the opening of the special session on the morning of 12 February, 2021, the UN Deputy High Commissioner for Human Rights told the Human Rights Council that the seizure of power by the military constituted a profound setback for the country, after a decade of hard-won gains in its democratic transition. Myanmar's democratically elected political leadership, including Aung San Suu Kyi and President U Win Myint, had been detained on politically motivated charges.

More than 350 political and state officials, activists and civil society members, including journalists, monks and students, she continued, had been taken into custody. Most had received no form of due process and had not been permitted legal representation, family visitations or communication. The Deputy High Commissioner continued:

> The world is watching. Draconian orders have been issued this week to prevent peaceful assembly and free expression, and police and military

> presence on the streets has grown progressively over the last several days. Following violent clashes with police on 9 February, at least one woman is in critical condition. Pro-military and nationalist groups have also taken to the streets.
>
> Let us be clear: the indiscriminate use of lethal or less-than-lethal weapons against peaceful protestors is unacceptable. More violence against Myanmar's people will only compound the illegitimacy of the coup, and the culpability of its leaders.[10]

The Human Rights Council's Special Rapporteur on the situation of human rights in Myanmar, Tom Andrews, speaking on his own behalf and also on behalf of the Coordinating Committee of Special Procedures [human rights investigators] of the Human Rights Council, told the Council that there was no justification for declaring a state of emergency, arresting the civilian leadership and attempting to destroy Myanmar's fledgling democracy. He urged: "As the people of Myanmar demonstrate their remarkable courage and resolve, let us demonstrate our support of them and the principles and values that they are fighting for."[11]

Following statements by the representative of Myanmar and other representatives, the Human Rights Council, without a vote, adopted a resolution calling urgently for the immediate and unconditional release of all persons arbitrarily detained in Myanmar, including State Counsellor Aung San Suu Kyi and President Win Myint and the lifting of the state of emergency.

The Council deplored the removal of the Government democratically elected by the people of Myanmar in the general election held on 8 November, 2020 and the suspension of mandates of all members of parliaments, and called for the restoration of the democratically elected government. The Council further called urgently for the immediate and unconditional release of all persons arbitrarily detained, and the lifting of the state of emergency. The Council stressed the need for the junta to refrain from violence and fully respect human rights, fundamental freedoms, and the rule of law.

The Council requested the UN High Commissioner for Human Rights and its Special Rapporteur on the situation of human rights in Myanmar to assess the prevailing human rights situation in Myanmar and to provide updates in

10 Special Session on the Human Rights Implications of the Crisis in Myanmar. Statement by Deputy High Commissioner for Human Rights Nada Al-Nashif, 12 February, 2021.

11 UH Press Release, 12 February, 2021: Deputy High Commissioner for Human Rights to the Special Session of the Human Rights Council on Myanmar: Seizure of Power by Military Constitutes a Profound Setback for Myanmar.

their reports to the Human Rights Council at its regular session due to begin later in February.[12]

In the debate preceding the adoption of the resolution, speakers said that censorship had been tightened in Myanmar and security forces had cracked down violently against peaceful protesters, in violation of international standards. They urged the Council to support all accountability mechanisms and any solutions for the peaceful resolution of the current situation. It should not be forgotten, they added, that there were reasons to believe that the military had committed crimes against humanity and possibly genocide. The warning signs were ominous: Myanmar risked returning to the days of mass incarceration of human rights defenders.

The representative of Myanmar told the Human Rights Council that the country was undergoing complex challenges and a delicate transition, and therefore looked forward to receiving better understanding on the prevailing situation in the country, and constructive engagement and cooperation from the international community.

Unfortunately, the efforts of the Council have so far had little impact on the situation on the ground.

3 Urgent Actions by the President of the Council

In the chapter on good offices below we discuss actions by the President of the Council for the protection of persons at risk of reprisals for exercising their human rights. At the opening of the 46th session of the Council, for example, the President, Nazhat Shameem Khan, told the Council that she would follow up on all allegations brought to her attention of acts of reprisal and intimidation committed against persons in connection with their contribution to the work of the Human Rights Council, its mechanisms and procedures.[13]

Here, we focus on other forms of urgent action by the President of the Council. In an email exchange with this author, for example, a recent President of the Council stated:

> Last year I spent weeks (including weekends) between April and June talking to colleagues in plenaries, groups and bilaterals to convince them to take up the work of the Human Rights Council again after the first

12 UN Press Release, Human Rights Council calls for release of all arbitrarily detained persons in Myanmar, and lifting of state of emergency, 12 February, 2021.

13 UN Press Release HRC/21/6 – 22 February, 2021.

COVID-19 lockdown. As a result, the Human Rights Council was the first body to do so and the only one in the UN system to complete its full programme of work. Quite a number of delegations had thought the pandemic might be a great opportunity for them to make the Human Rights Council go silent for a while. We thwarted that by finding answers to all their health risk arguments and the corresponding modalities were then taken over by other UN bodies.[14]

4 Urgent Actions by the High Commissioner at the Request of the Council

On 17 June, 2020, the Human Rights Council held an urgent debate on racially inspired human rights violations, systemic racism, police brutality and violence against peaceful protesters. The murder of George Floyd, an African-American man, by a law enforcement official on 25 May 2020 in Minnesota, United States, had sparked world-wide protests. The Council eventually adopted a resolution, 43/1, requesting High Commissioner, Michelle Bachelet, to prepare a comprehensive report on systemic racism and violations of international human rights law against Africans and people of African descent by law enforcement agencies. The Council also asked the High Commissioner to study related issues of accountability and redress, as well as Government responses to anti-racism peaceful protests.

In the report that she submitted to the Council, High Commissioner Bachelet offered an agenda to dismantle systematic racism. She called for action to "reverse cultures of denial, dismantle systemic racism and accelerate the pace of action." The report called on States to right historic wrongs, while addressing the current realities and lived experiences of people of African descent.[15]

5 Conclusion

One would have to give a measure of credit to the Council for its special sessions that deal with emergency situations. The urgent appeals of the Council's special procedures mandate-holders also deserve credit. Whether on behalf of

14 E-mail to the author dated 24 February, 2021. For reasons of discretion we do not refer to the name of the President.

15 See, OHCHR, "Seminal UN report offers an agenda to dismantle systemic racism", https://www.ohchr.org?EN/NewsEvents/Pages/systemic-=_racism.aspx, 29 June, 2021.

the Council, or on her own volition, the High Commissioner for Human Rights does try to place the spotlight on the plight of victims in need of support and corrective action.

Yet, there is a simple, inescapable fact: there are numerous victims, and numerous emergency situations that receive no attention by, or on behalf of the Council. Until the Council rises to this standard, it must be considered as failing the victims of gross violations of human rights who deserve its urgent attention.

As we discussed in an earlier chapter, the protection of human rights should be preventive, mitigatory, and remedial. The leading human rights organ of the United Nations should have a well-developed policy of urgent action to respond to the needs of persons at risk, or persons whose rights are being violated. Special sessions of the Council are, admittedly, a worthwhile form of urgent action. But it is not enough.

Neither the President nor the Bureau of the Council has so far developed an urgent-action role. The void is left to be filled by the High Commissioner and by Special Procedures mandate-holders. As we saw from the distressing report submitted to the Council by the Special Rapporteur against torture, governments are far from acting in good faith when responding to urgent action representations by Special Procedures.

We would have to conclude that, for the time being, alas, the urgent-action role of the Council remains limited.

CHAPTER 6

Good Offices

1 Introduction

Gross violations of human rights continue to be numerous across the world and the victims are often without any protection nationally, regionally or internationally. This is a sad reality of the human condition in our times. Good offices are a long-standing feature of the practice of the United Nations to help human beings in distress. Historically, this kind of good offices has been exercised by the UN Secretary-General, the President of the UN General Assembly, the President of the Security Council, the head of the UN human rights programme, now the UN High Commissioner for Human Rights, the Chairpersons of UN human rights treaty bodies, the Chairpersons of the former Commission on Human Rights and now, since the Human Rights Council took over from the Commission in 2006, by the President of the Human Rights Council.[1] In this chapter, we shall look at three contexts of the exercise of good offices under the auspices of the Council: urgent communications to Governments from human rights mandate-holders, known as special procedures; the confidential complaints procedure in the Council; and action by the President of the Council for the protection of human rights defenders at risk.

2 Urgent Communications to Governments

The Human Rights Council inherited from its predecessor, and has continued and expanded, a system of 'special procedures': investigators and analysts mandated to act for the protection of human rights. In 2020, special procedure mandate holders presented 134 reports to the Human Rights Council and 48 reports to the General Assembly.[2] Special procedures mandate holders regularly present to the Council reports on urgent action representations made to Governments.[3]

---

1 See for a historical perspective, Bertrand G. Ramcharan, Humanitarian Good Offices in International Law. The Good Offices of the UN Secretary-General in the Field of Human Rights. The Hague, Martinus Nijhoff, 1983.

2 See UN doc. A/HRC/46/24: Conclusions and recommendations of special procedures: Report of the Secretary-General.

3 Ibid, para. 89.

 | DOI:10.1163/9789004504950_008

The website of the Office of High Commissioner for Human Rights carries a document, "Communications sent report", consulted on 27 February, 2021, which shows that in 2020 special procedures mandate holders sent 368 communications to Governments. The following is a random selection from this report taken from the months of June and November, 2020.

On 2 June, 2020, several special procedures mandate holders transmitted to the Government of Angola information received concerning acts of intimidation and harassment of human rights defenders working for the non-governmental organization MBAKITA. The same day, several special procedures mandate holders transmitted to the Government of China information received concerning the continued enforced disappearance of Gedhun Cheokyi Nuima, who had allegedly been made to disappear twenty-five years earlier. The information transmission also included allegations of harassment against the religious traditions and practices of the Tibetan Buddhist minority.

On 2 June, also, several special procedures mandate holders transmitted to the Government of Egypt information received concerning the arrest and ongoing pre-trial detention of prominent labour rights activists and trade union leaders, including Haytham Mohammedein, Hassan Barbary, Alla Essam and Khalil Rizk. On 2 June, several special procedures mandate holders transmitted to the Government of Iran information received expressing concerns about the criteria for temporary release of prisoners due to the COVID – 19 pandemic.

On 2 June, several special procedures mandate holders transmitted to the Government of Saudi Arabia information received regarding the continued detention of five women human rights defenders and the death in prison of human rights defender Mr Abdullah Hamid Al-Hamid. The same day, several special procedures mandate holders transmitted to the Government of Zimbabwe information received concerning the arbitrary arrest, disappearance, torture and ill-treatment of members of the MDC Alliance Youth Assembly.

On 3 June, 2020, several special procedures mandate holders transmitted to the Government of South Africa information received concerning alleged verbal and physical assaults by police officers against journalist Mr Paul Nthiobia. The same day, two special procedures mandate holders sent to the Government of Zimbabwe information received concerning the arrest and excessive use of force against human rights defender Gamichurai Mukura.

On 27 November, 2020, several special procedures mandate holders sent a communication to the Government of Iraq transmitting information concerning the alleged arbitrary detention of journalist Mr Sherwan Amin Naao Sherwani. The same day, several special procedures mandate holders sent a communication to the Government of Myanmar transmitting information received concerning the alleged arbitrary arrest and detention of an environmental human rights defender in Chin State, Myanmar. That day, also, several special procedures mandate holders sent a communication to the Government of Peru transmitting information on alleged assassinations, intimidation, harassment and kidnapping of indigenous leaders and human rights defenders.

On 25 November, several special procedures mandate holders sent a communication to the Government of Ivory Coast transmitting information on the alleged arbitrary detention and enforced disappearance of a number of named persons as well as restrictions on the right to peaceful assembly.

On 25 November, also, several special procedures mandate holders sent to the Government of Egypt a communication concerning the arrest and filing of charges for terrorism and national security-related crimes against three named human rights defenders, in apparent retaliation for a human rights meeting they had held with representatives of the diplomatic community, under the auspices of the NGO, the Egyptian Initiative for Personal Rights (EIPR). The Special Procedures mandate-holders added: "We also bring to the attention of Your Excellency's Government information regarding the continued pre-trial detention of another EIPR staff, Patrick Zaki as well as the ongoing criminalization, travel ban and freeze of assets of Hossam Baghat, founder and former Executive Director of the same organization."

On 25 November, several special procedures mandate holders sent to the Government of Guinea information received concerning allegations of acts of violence and incitement of hatred and violence in media controlled by the ruling leaders during an electoral campaign. On the same date, several special procedures mandate holders transmitted to the Government of Myanmar allegations received on the targeting and intimidation of a Rohingya human rights defender living in the United Kingdom. The same information was also transmitted to the government of the United Kingdom.

On 20 November, several special procedures mandate holders sent to the Government of Colombia information received concerning four 'trans' women from Venezuela who had allegedly been detained arbitrarily by the Colombian police. On 20 November, also, the special rapporteur on the independence of judges and lawyers transmitted to the Government of Haiti information received concerning the alleged murder of Mr Monferrier Dorval who had allegedly been killed because of positions he had taken in the practice of his profession as a lawyer.

It is not straightforward to assess the results of such urgent actions by special procedures mandate holders. Governments often simply deny the allegations in question or provide alleged grounds for the treatment of the persons concerned. The hope of the special procedures mandate holders is that transmitting the information would put Governments on notice that their actions are being monitored by the international community. It would also be hoped that Governments might stop or reduce the violations. In some instances, Governments of good faith might act to release a detainee or otherwise provide humanitarian relief. This is the nature of the human rights endeavour: one does what is possible in the circumstances to help people undergoing violations or at risk of them.

3 Confidential Complaints Procedure

In 1970 the ECOSOC established a procedure according to which petitions received by the Secretariat were listed and then forwarded to the Governments concerned for their information and comments. The Commission on Human Rights also received authorization to act on situations dealt with in these petitions that revealed a 'consistent pattern of gross violations of human right'. Between 1970 and 2006, when the Commission on Human Rights gave way to the present Human Rights Council, some eighty four country situations were examined in the Commission.

The bulk of petitions received by the human rights secretariat were processed in accordance with a procedure laid down by ECOSOC resolution 1503 (XLVIII) of 27 May, 1970.Underthis procedure, the Commission on Human Rights, after examining situations involving an alleged consistent pattern of reliably-attested gross violations of human rights, could determine:

> Whether it required a thorough study by the Commission and a report and recommendations thereon to the ECOSOC.
>
> Whether it might be the subject of an investigation by an *ad hoc* committee to be appointed by the Commission. Such a study was to be undertaken only with the express consent of the State concerned and to be conducted in constant cooperation with that State.

The Commission took one of the following three courses of action in dealing with these situations: first, representatives of the Governments accused were invited for a confidential discussion in the Commission, and this could take place over successive sessions if the Commission kept the situation under discussion. Second, the Commission occasionally sent an emissary, an "independent expert" designated by itself or the Secretary-General for 'direct contacts' with the Government concerned in the early years, and, later, with the government and the people of the country, and to draw up a report on those contacts. Third, the Commission sometimes asked the Secretariat to extend advisory services and technical assistance to the Government concerned to help it improve its national human rights laws and infrastructure. Occasionally, the Commission might move the consideration of the situation involved into public sessions and even adopt resolutions critical of the government.

These were not spectacular actions, but they could be meaningful. Dictatorships such as those in Argentina, Chile, Equatorial Guinea, Ethiopia, Haiti, the Philippines, Uganda, Uruguay, and Uzbekistan invariably sought to denounce their accusers and to obstruct the procedures. In one instance, that of Uganda, its Attorney-General vigorously defended his government against allegations of mass slaughter and then, the week after, defected in London and denounced the Government of Idi Amin Dada!

A UN Under-Secretary-General, Davidson Nichol, entrusted with the task of engaging in direct contacts with the President of Ethiopia, Menghistu Haile Mariam, had to meet him in his military tank at night, as he slept in different locations in Addis Ababa. Mr Nichol submitted a thoughtful report to the Commission expressing concern about the situation in Ethiopia. A former Judge of the International Court of Justice, Mr Justice Onyeama, was entrusted with the task of undertaking "a thorough study" of the human rights situation in Uganda, where the government had liquidated a quarter of a million of its people. He met with prevarications and obstruction. The mandate of Justice Onyeama was discontinued following the fall of Idi Amin.

A highly decorated World-War II hero from Canada, Michel Gauvin, undertook direct contacts with the Government of Haiti in Port-au-Prince. He submitted a detailed report to the Commission which was subsequently made public. He made a number of recommendations to help improve the situation and was followed by a succession of emissaries to Haiti later on.

A Professor from Costa Rica, Fernando Volio-Jimenez, undertook direct contact missions to Equatorial Guinea. This is now an oil-rich country, but in his first report Volio-Jimenez reported that in those days it lacked a printing press to print the laws it enacted. He recommended advisory services and technical assistance.

Javier Perez de Cuellar, then an Under-Secretary-General, who later became UN Secretary-General, was mandated to undertake direct contact missions to Paraguay and Uruguay. He was able to visit Uruguay and submitted a brief report to the Commission. Professor Sadako Ogata, later to become UN High Commissioner for Refugees, undertook a mission to the then Burma, now Myanmar, and submitted thoughtful reports to the Commission. She was succeeded in that mandate by Professor Yozo Yokota, who also reported to the Commission.

What did actions such as these signify? The most important significance for people on the ground was that they knew that the UN was visiting their country and talking to the Government and leading members of society about the situation. This gave them hope, even if the situation did not immediately improve. In one instance, colleagues in the human rights secretariat noted that the number of allegations of torture in Uruguay that had been numerous, gradually came to an end.

And after the restoration of democracy in countries such as Argentina, Paraguay and Uruguay, the new democratic governments requested that the petitions, records of discussions in the Commission, and other confidential documents that had been before the Commission in closed session under a confidential procedure be made public. These materials were subsequently used in trials against alleged violators in these countries. The records of the Commission under this procedure became parts of the history of these countries.

The confidential petitions procedure described above also led to thousands of people from Eastern European countries being allowed to emigrate to their freedom. This came about in the following circumstances: When petitions were received they were transmitted to the Governments concerned for their information and response. Formally, the Governments declined to respond. Unannounced, however, a number of countries in Eastern Europe such as Bulgaria, the GDR and Romania, in response to the petitions submitted to the United Nations, quietly allowed many petitioners to emigrate to freedom abroad.

After emigrating to their new countries in freedom, numerous petitioners wrote "Thank You" letters to the United Nations, expressing gratitude for the role of the Organization in helping secure their freedom. The petitions branch of the human rights secretariat kept a "Thank You" file containing these letters. Unfortunately, when the human rights secretariat moved from the Palais des Nations in Geneva to the Palais Wilson the human rights secretariat was only allowed by the leadership to take a limited amount of the archives and the "Thank You" file passed into history.

When the Human Rights Council replaced the former Commission on Human Rights in 2006 it continued a modified confidential complaints procedure with one manor change: under the procedure operated by the former Commission on Human Rights, the selection of situations for consideration was done by a group of expert members of its Sub-Commission on human rights. In contrast, in the Human Rights Council the selection of situations is now done by a group of Members of the Council and the political element in the selection and handling of situations thus became prominent.

The website of the Office of High Commissioner for Human Rights has a "List of Situations Referred to the Human Rights Council under the Complaints Procedure Since 2006." It carries information for the years between 2006 and 2014, but, as of February, 2021, had not been updated for the period after 2014.

According to the list, in 2006, the Council considered the situation of human rights in Kyrgyzstan and adopted a decision encouraging the Government to continue its efforts in an effective and timely manner. The Council then discontinued its consideration of the situation. In 2007, the Council decided to discontinue consideration of the human rights situation in Uzbekistan and also to discontinue consideration of the situation in Iran. In 2008, the Council decided to discontinue consideration of the human rights situation in the Maldives.

In 2008, the Council decided to keep the human rights situation in Turkmenistan under review but the next year, 2009, the Council decided to discontinue consideration of that situation. In 2009, the Council decided the keep the human rights situation in Guinea under review. It also decided to discontinue consideration of the human rights situation in the Democratic Republic of the Congo. In 2009, also, the Council decided to keep the human rights situation in Guinea under review. In 2010, the Council decided to discontinue considering the human rights situation in Guinea.

In 2011, the Council decided to keep the human rights situation in Tajikistan under review but later that year it decided to discontinue its consideration of the situation. In 2011, also, the Council decided to keep under review the human rights situation in the Democratic Republic of the Congo, as well as to recommend that the Office of the High Commissioner for Human Rights provide the Government with technical cooperation, capacity-building assistance or advisory services as needed in the situations examined under the Complaints procedure.

In 2012, the Council decided to discontinue consideration of the human rights situation in Turkmenistan. That same year, 2012, the Council decided to discontinue consideration of the human rights situation in the Democratic Republic of the Congo. Further still, in 2012, the Council decided to keep under review its consideration of the situation of human rights in Iraq. Later that year it decided to discontinue consideration of the situation and recommended that the Office of High Commissioner for Human Rights increase technical cooperation, capacity building, assistance and advisory services to Iraq. Later still, in the same year, the Council decided "to discontinue consideration of the situation of trade unions and their members and leaders, as well as human rights defenders in Iraq."

In 2012, the Council decided to discontinue reviewing the human rights situation in Eritrea under its confidential complaint procedure in order to take up public consideration of the same situation. The Council also decided that the documentation that it had considered relating to the situation in Eritrea under its confidential complaints procedure should no longer be considered confidential, with the exception of the names or any other identifying information of specific individuals who had not consented, and should therefore be transmitted to the Council's newly appointed Special Rapporteur on the situation of human rights in Eritrea.

The Council invited the Special Rapporteur to investigate further the allegations "contained in the submitted complaints and the circumstances of the individuals mentioned in the submitted communications whose names may be disclosed … and to report thereon to the Human Rights Council at its twenty-third session." The Council urged the Government of Eritrea to cooperate fully with the Special Rapporteur, in particular to permit access to visit all parts of the country and to provide the information."

In 2014, the Council decided, at its 25th session, to keep under review the human rights situation in Cameroon until its twenty-seventh situation.

From the foregoing it will be seen that in the nine years between 2006 and 2014, the Council considered the situation of nine countries in confidential procedure: Kyrgyzstan, Uzbekistan, Maldives, Turkmenistan, Guinea, Democratic Republic of the Congo, Iraq, Eritrea and Cameroon. The representatives of these nine countries would have been invited for confidential discussions with members of the Council. Those representatives would have informed their Governments in capitals that human rights issues inside their countries were receiving scrutiny within the Council. This, hopefully, might have had some mitigating effect on the behaviour of those Governments, although this should not be assumed. In two instances, the Council asked the Office of High Commissioner to offer advisory services and technical assistance. The OHCHR "List" does not refer to any envoys being sent to Government capitals for discussions on the ground.

4 Good Offices by the President of the Human Rights Council

Goof offices have historically been exercised by the Chairpersons of the former Commission on Human Rights and now by the Presidents of its successor, the Human Rights Council. The Chairpersons of the former

Commission on Human Rights, starting with Mrs Eleanor Roosevelt, sought, in some instances, when circumstances permitted it, to use their personal influence to help people undergoing, or at risk of, gross violations of human rights. Mrs Roosevelt played a crucial role in steering the Commission on Human Rights towards the adoption of the Universal Declaration of Human Rights. Mrs Roosevelt was moved by the plight of women in the world and by the injustices against Afro-Americans in the USA, and sought to get UN norms adopted against discrimination being experienced by women and by Afro-Americans.

The Commission on Human Rights operated from 1947 to 1989 under the shadow of the Cold War and the room for action by the Chairperson was thereby circumscribed. Nevertheless, Chairpersons of the Commission did, on occasions, act behind the scenes when they could do so on behalf of victims of human rights violations. The late Felix Ermacora of Austria, for example, believed in a role for the Chairperson between the annual sessions of the Commission and he did seek to bring his influence to bear on situations arising while the Commission was not in session. He contacted Permanent Representatives and sometimes contacted Governments in capitals.[4]

The late Waleed Saadi of Jordan also believed in an inter-sessional role for the Chair of the Commission and he, like Felix Ermacora, made representations from time to time to Permanent Representatives and Government officials in capitals. Ambassador Saadi acted in relation to the situation of disappeared persons in Chile, urging Government representatives to cooperate in investigations by appointees of the Commission into the fate of missing persons.[5]

The late Keba M'Baye of Senegal sought to exercise his good offices in respect of human rights situations then prevailing in Haiti and Uganda, and also played an active part in discussing with Government representatives measures that could be taken to ameliorate other troubling human rights situations brought up under the confidential petitions procedure established by ECOSOC resolution 1503 (XLVIII).

The late Yvonne Beaulne of Canada took a particular interest in the phenomenon of enforced and involuntary disappearances that was prevalent in Latin America while he served as Chairperson. He engaged in diplomatic contacts with Government representatives, notably those of Argentina, Chile

4 This is based on conversations the author had with the late Prof. Ermacora.

5 The author worked closely with the late Ambassador Saadi during his chairpersonship. Ambassador Saadi discussed with him the Ambassador's thoughts on the inter-sessional role of the Chairperson.

and Uruguay. He developed a close relationship with the Representative of Uruguay, Ambassador Giancarlo Giambruno, and he passed on to him cases in which he sought protection of individuals at risk. He also sought to use his influence to advance the human rights cause in Equatorial Guinea, which was then being examined under the '1503 procedure'.

From the inception of the Human Rights Council in 2006, its President has used his or her good offices to help attenuate human rights violations. The first President of the Council, Luis Alfonso de Alba played a personal role in negotiating the establishment of a High Level Panel on the situation in Darfur. At the time there were allegations of genocide being committed in Darfur. It would be fair to say that, but for the efforts of President de Alba, the Panel would not have been established nor been able to operate, albeit in the face of strenuous opposition by the then Government of Sudan and its allies on the Council. President de Alba appointed this author as a member of the Panel and discussed his vision with the author at the time.

Presidents of the Council after de Alba have similarly played a role in facilitating the establishment and functioning of commissions of inquiry into situations of international concern such as those in Syria and Myanmar. Presidents of the Council have also regularly performed a good offices function on behalf of the protection of human rights defenders at risk of reprisal.

The UN Secretary-General has mandated the Assistant-Secretary-General for Human Rights in charge of the New York secretariat of the Office of High Commissioner for Human Rights with the task of serving as a focal point in cases of alleged reprisals against human rights defenders. The Assistant Secretary-General submits an annual written report to the Human Rights Council and presents it annually to the Council. The report and its presentation are discussed in the Council and sometimes Members of the Council in a position to do so make urgent appeals to Governments to help protect those at risk.

The President of the Council, since the establishment of the Council, has sought to use his or her good offices on behalf of persons at risk of reprisals. During the Nigerian Presidency of the Council, a Colombian human rights advocate came to Geneva to make representations about human rights issues involving indigenous peoples. As she was on her way back to Colombia, her husband was shot and killed and this was considered a clear act of reprisal. The President, Ambassador Martin Uhomoibhi, who was widely respected, summoned the Colombian Ambassador and denounced the killing. He asked for, and received, assurances on the safety and security of the NGO representative. He followed this up in the Council itself where he sought and obtained assurances from the Colombian Representative that no further reprisal would be taken against the NGO delegate. He continued to monitor this situation for the duration of his Presidency. Ambassador Uhomoibhi also acted similarly in respect of a human rights defender under threat in the Gambia.[6]

In an email exchange with this author, a former President of the Council stated the following:

> During my Presidency I talked to some 10–12 Ambassadors on reported cases of reprisals which had been checked by OHCHR beforehand on their plausibility … All of them said there must have been some sort of misunderstanding and that the facts were different. Some of them sent me lengthy information material from their capitals pointing out that there was a risk for their country's 'security'. They were all very polite, diplomatic and civilized – except for the final case of the year … The Ambassador wrote to me twice that this was none of my business. The second letter came after I had explained that reacting to reprisals was the responsibility of the President of the Human Rights Council and that all my predecessors had done so according to a pre-established procedure.[7]

5 Conclusion

Three things stand out from this chapter: first, during 2020, 368 urgent communications were sent to Governments by mandate-holders of the Human Rights Council urging those Governments to act for the protection of the human rights of persons who seemed to be at risk and to take corrective measures to prevent gross violations of human rights that seemed imminent. Second, the Human Rights Council operates a confidential complaints procedure under which it dialogues annually with the representatives of one or more Governments in an effort to bring about improvements in the human rights situation in the countries involved. Third, the President of the Council sometimes intercedes with Governments seeking the protection of human rights defenders at risk of reprisal. One cannot assess the results of these actions and whether they actually contribute to protecting the human rights of persons at risk. But the actions taken do represent good faith striving by mandate-holders, Members,

6 I am grateful to Peter Splinter, former Representative of Amnesty International in Geneva for bringing these two cases to my attention.

7 This email correspondence took place in 2021. For purposes of discretion, we do not name the President involved. We are grateful to the former President for sharing her insights.

and the President to help people undergoing violations, or at risk of violations. It is without doubt an unjust world that experiences these gross violations of human rights. But, through the exercise of good offices, there is striving, in good faith, to help people in distress, or at risk.

CHAPTER 7

Fact-Finding

1 Introduction

Fact-finding is the crown jewel within the Human Rights Council. Technically, it is sometimes not without its flaws, and has been criticized on occasion for alleged partiality. Human rights fact-finders appointed by the Council, popularly known as its Special Procedures, have come under political pressure by Members of the Council to engage in more dialogue and cooperation and less 'confrontation'. The Council, early on, adopted a Code of Conduct for its fact-finders, the first draft of which was quite draconian. Nevertheless, each year, some fifty human rights special procedures of the Council gather and assess information from all parts of the world about grievous human rights violations, visit countries to probe into allegations, make urgent appeals to Governments to protect those at risk, write and publish thousands of pages of fact-finding reports, and report in person to the Council during its regular sessions, when their work is examined by the Members of the Council. Taken together, the reports of these fact-finders represent the nearest thing to a global human rights report detailing human rights violations such as arbitrary, summary and extra-judicial killings, torture, enforced and involuntary disappearances, human trafficking, violence against women, exploitation of children, and other shocking violations of human rights.

In addition to the special procedures, the Council sometimes appoints Commissions of Inquiry into situations of alleged gross violations of human rights. Invariably, their reports are criticized by the government concerned. Sometimes they may indeed have flaws. But for the most part, their reports represent good faith efforts of conscience and, often, their reports are of great quality amounting to no less than historical records of shocking gross violations of human rights in the situations concerned. The report of the Commission of Inquiry into allegations of widespread human rights violations in the Democratic People's Republic of Korea, was an example of a gold standard investigation that called on the UN Security Council to refer the allegations to the International Criminal Court.

The Council is pressed for time and usually allots about three hours each for the presentation and discussion of the reports of special procedures mandate-holders. It cannot be said that the Council devotes to these reports the detailed attention they deserve. Members and Observers are able to participate in the

 | DOI:10.1163/9789004504950_009

discussion, including some NGOs. Resolutions adopted by the Council after its discussion of these reports vary in detailed focus and in the follow-up given to the various allegations of gross violations presented. It often depends on what can be negotiated as a resolution within the Membership of the Council. The publicity given to these reports by the UN and by the media is little. But human rights organizations within the countries concerned may be able to publicise and capitalize on these reports in their quest for justice. And the victims take heart from the fact that violations have been documented and presented to the world human rights body. If democracy and fair governance returns to the country concerned, reports of UN human rights fact-finders may be used to draw lessons for the future, or evidence therein can be marshalled before the courts in trials of the perpetrators. This took place in the past in countries such as Argentina, Chile, and Uruguay.[1]

Put simply, human rights fact-finding within the framework of the Human Rights Council represents the best efforts that the international community is able to marshal to document gross violations of human rights the world over and to strive for the protection of the victims, actual and potential. It is not perfect. The violations and problems to be addressed are numerous indeed and the world, as it is, is itself quite imperfect. But human rights fact-finding within the Council represents 'striving' by the international community for greater justice. In this chapter we shall discuss the efforts of the human rights special procedures, commissions of inquiry and similar exercises.

2 Principles of Fact-Finding

The Council has adopted a Code of Conduct for its Special Procedures mandate-holders. These principles emerged out of an initial effort to strictly control and curtail the room for maneuver of the mandate holders.

Since its establishment the Council has established numerous fact-finding groups. Based on the practice of these groups, the Office of High Commissioner for Human Rights published an extensive study on Commissions of Inquiry and Fact-Finding Missions on International Human Rights and Humanitarian Law: Guidance and Practice.[2] Based on its study of their practice, the OHCHR

1 These involved reports of special procedures of the Human Rights Council's predecessor, the Commission on Human Rights.

2 United Nations, OHCHR, New York and Geneva, 2015.

presented the following *Principles of human rights and international humanitarian law fact-finding and investigation*:[3]

2.1 *Do No Harm*

While the commission/mission is unable to guarantee the safety of the persons it comes into contact with, it should ensure that its actions or inactions do not jeopardize the safety of such persons, its staff, its information or its work. It should also ensure that its activities are not detrimental to the United Nations.

2.2 *Independence*

Members and staff of the commission/mission are required to act independently. They should ensure that they do not seek or accept instructions from any person, Government or other source, and are not unduly influenced in the exercise of their functions by any person, Government, NGO or other entity.

2.3 *Impartiality*

All tasks of the commission/mission should be based on its mandate and applicable international norms, and alleged violations by all parties should be investigated with equal thoroughness and vigour. The commission/mission should avoid any perception that it could be siding with one party over another.

2.4 *Transparency*

The commission/mission should, as far as possible without detriment to its work, or the security of its staff, information and persons cooperating with it, make information about its mandate, methodology and work publicly available. Commissions/missions do not work in secrecy and undertake activities in a country only with the consent of the Government.

2.5 *Objectivity*

The commission/mission is required to collect all relevant facts from all relevant sources, objectively consider all the facts and information gathered and base its conclusions on the facts gathered. It should take into consideration only information that is gathered in an unbiased and impartial manner.

3 Ibid, pp. 33-35.

2.6 *Confidentiality*

The commission/mission is required to respect the confidentiality of persons who cooperate with it and of the information it gathers. In addition to the protection it affords, confidentiality enhances the credibility of the commission/mission, the integrity of its information-gathering activities and the effectiveness of its work.

2.7 *Credibility*

The commission/mission needs to gain the trust of victims, witnesses and others to obtain their cooperation in providing information. It should not make any promises it is unlikely to fulfil and should follow through on any promises it does make.

2.8 *Visibility*

The Commission/mission should have a visible presence in the country concerned, if it is granted access. This makes the authorities aware of its work, and allows victims and witnesses to approach it with information. Visibility could also deter further human rights violations. However, the commission/mission should be aware that visibility could also present risks to persons wanting to cooperate with it, and should take appropriate precautions.

2.9 *Integrity*

The commission/mission should treat all victims, witnesses and other cooperative persons with decency and respect. It should be respectful in its dealings with government authorities and alleged perpetrators. Members and staff should act with honesty. They should also ensure that the commission's/mission's investigation methodology guarantees the integrity of the process of collecting, evaluating and analysing information, and is beyond reproach.

2.10 *Professionalism*

Members and staff are required to approach each task in a professional manner with the required knowledge, diligence and competence.

2.11 *Consistency*

The commission/mission should examine and analyse each piece of information it receives, irrespective of the source. It should continue this process until it has completed a thorough and comprehensive inquiry, all possible sources of information have been explored and it has obtained a clear understanding of the situation under investigation.

Although the foregoing principles emanated from its Secretariat, the OHCHR, and have not been formally approved by the Council, they make be taken as a reasonable codification of the principles of fact-finding that have emerged in the practice of commissions/missions established by the Council and, to that extent, part of its jurisprudence. This buttressed by the following statement at the end of the foregoing principles: "The international standards, principles and guidance on methods of work can be found in international human rights treaties, United Nations declarations and principles, and United Nations manuals and guidelines "[4]

3 The Special Procedures and Commissions of Inquiry

There is important fact-finding activity of high quality that takes place under the auspices of the Human Rights Council. The Council's Commission on Human Rights in South Sudan is an example of this quality fact-finding. The Council established the Commission at its thirty-first session and subsequently renewed its mandate annually, requesting it to monitor and report on the situation of human rights in South Sudan, to make recommendations to prevent further deterioration of the situation, and to report and provide guidance on transitional justice, including reconciliation.

The Council also requested the Commission to determine and report the facts and circumstances of, to collect and preserve evidence of, and to clarify responsibility for alleged gross violations and abuses of human rights and related crimes, including sexual and gender-based violence and ethnic violence, with a view to ending impunity and providing accountability. The Council further requested the Commission to make such information available to all transitional justice mechanisms, including those to be established pursuant to chapter V of the Agreement on the Resolution of the Conflict in South Sudan, including the hybrid court for South Sudan to be established in cooperation with the African Union.

As of the time of writing, the members of the Commission, appointed by the President of the Council, were Yasmin Sooka (Chair), Andrew Clapham and Barney Afako. In its report to the 46th session of the Council, the Commission reported that it was being supported by a secretariat based in Juba, South Sudan.[5] It conducted missions to several locations within South Sudan and

4 Ibid, p. 35.

5 A/HRC/46/533.

also conducted missions in Europe (undisclosed locations). The Commission met with a wide range of victims, witnesses, government officials, members of civil society and other key stakeholders.

During its current mandate, as reported to the Council, the Commission took more than 100 detailed individual witness statements and gathered more than 100 documents, including confidential records covering incidents in South Sudan since December, 2013. All the evidence collected was preserved in the Commission's confidential database and archives.

In the light of the mandate's emphasis on accountability, the Commission also focused on establishing responsibility for violations and identifying individuals bearing responsibility for those violations and crimes. To clarify responsibility for international crimes, in particular, command or superior responsibility under international law, the Commission sought to identify command structures, patterns of conduct and indicators of control and discipline.

The Commission adopted a 'reasonable grounds to believe' evidentiary standard. Its work was informed by the requirement to collect and preserve evidence to a standard that would support future accountability mechanisms, including criminal responsibility. Where the Commission found information linking alleged perpetrators to specific violations or to patterns of violations that was sufficient to warrant future criminal investigations or prosecutions, such information was retained on a strictly confidential basis. In some instances, there was insufficient information to identify individuals responsible for violations; in such cases, the armed forces or armed groups to which those individuals belonged had been identified as responsible.

"The Commission employed best practices of fact-finding aimed at assuring the safety, security, confidentiality and well-being of witnesses. Accordingly, information has been included only where sources granted informed consent and where disclosure would not lead to the identification of sources or result in harm … The Commission was at all times guided by the principle of 'do no harm'."[6]

In its report to the 46th session of the Human Rights Council, the Commission concluded:

> "76. On the basis of its findings, the Commission has reasonable grounds to believe that members of the Government of South Sudan have engaged in acts amounting to gross human rights violations and serious violations of international humanitarian law in the context of the armed conflict

6 Ibid, paras 1-13, at para. 13.

in Central Equatoria. Government forces have also failed to respect their obligation to respect the right to food and freedom from hunger generally, in accordance with articles 9 (3) and 11 of the Transitional Constitution of South Sudan. The Government has also been complicit in gross human rights violations and abuses by arming and supporting organized militia groups during localized conflicts in Jonglei State, the Greater Pibor Administrative Area and Warrap State.

"77. At the subnational level, localized conflicts, often with the participation of organized armed militias affiliated with the South Sudan People's Defence Forces (SSPDF) or the Sudan People's Liberation Army in Opposition (SPLA-IO), were characterized by brutal attacks. Violations against civilians included abductions, including of children, murder, rape and other forms of sexual violence, physical and psychological torture and ill-treatment, looting and the destruction of civilian property, crops and other means of livelihood.

"78. In Central Equatoria, incidents of sexual and gender-based violence, including conflict-related violence, continued to be widespread and pervasive, including in the context of localized conflicts, and were characterized by a pattern of terror and subjugation. Violations documented by the Commission included rape and gang rape, sexual mutilation, forced marriage, abduction and sexualized torture. Children, including young girls, were also victims of sexual exploitation.

"79. Arbitrary arrests and detentions, and other restrictions on freedom of expression, opinion and assembly, also continued to characterize daily life in South Sudan, in acts that violated the right to information and expression, and freedom of association and assembly under the African Charter on Human and People's Rights. In addition, South Sudan, through continued acts of enforced disappearances, failed in its duty to investigate in good faith all allegations of human rights violations, in particular where the authorities alone had relevant information.

"80. Localized conflict also continued to pose a massive risk to stability in South Sudan, given the lack of accountability for gross violations and abuses and violations of international humanitarian law. The risk to stability is compounded by weak State structures, including at the subnational level, predatory elites and their competition for political power and economic resources, as well as the failure to manage ethnic division and plurality."

The Commission made detailed recommendations for actions needed to correct the situation described above. These included the following:

"(f) Finalize the process for the adoption of the memorandum of understanding with the African Union to facilitate and expedite the establishment of the hybrid court and the commission for truth, reconciliation and healing.

4 Conclusion

US Secretary-of-State Antony Blinken struck the right note when he assessed that the "Council plays a meaningful role in protecting human rights and fundamental freedoms by documenting atrocities in order to hold wrongdoers accountable"[7] Yes, the special procedures mandate-holders, commissions of inquiry, and the High Commissioner for Human Rights do assemble an impressive amount of data on gross violations of human rights in different parts of the world.

But the sad reality is that the Council often simply glosses over this data. And the data is not assembled together by anyone into a kind of world report on gross violations of human rights. So the cycle recurs annually and some issues get attention, while others do not. Fact-finding sometimes gets a meaningful response; but often it does not. This may be a consequence of the volume of gross violations of human rights in the world. But as the lead human rights organization of the United Nations, the Council has a duty to do better in responding to information presented to it about serious, gross violations of human rights that, alas, are prevalent in the world.

7 Statement issued by the US Department of State on the election of the United States of America to the Human Rights Council, 14 October, 2021.

CHAPTER 8

Redress

1 Introduction

At the end of the day, the sad fact is that there is little by way of redress in the activities of the Human Rights Council. Human rights NGOs often plead with the Council to pursue redress for victims of gross violations of human rights. Sometimes, the Council acts on such calls and many times it does not. One form of redress that the Council occasionally engages in, depending on the situation and on the attitude of the voting majority, is to express concern over, or condemn, gross violations of human rights. For the victims, this can give a bit of satisfaction. However, the prevailing mantra in the Council, even when dealing with situations of gross violations of human rights, is to engage in dialogue and cooperation, which often means that the Council is often not forthright in condemning gross violations of human rights and may, indeed, do so selectively.

Israel claims that the Council is prejudiced against it inasmuch as it frequently condemns Israel for alleged gross violations of human rights in occupied Palestine but does not similarly condemn other violators. It would be fair to concede that the Council does not condemn many governments deserving of such condemnation – leaving aside whether or not the condemnations of Israel in specific instances are well-founded or not.

Having recognized that redress in the Human Rights Council is selective and imperfect, our task in this chapter is to look first at the principles of redress and then to identify instances in which the Council may be considered to have pursued redress in particular situations. Based on the work of the Council's predecessor, the Commission on Human Rights, the General Assembly had adopted a set of principles on redress and compensation for victims of gross violations of human rights. We shall set out those principles by which, we think, the Council should be judged. Then we shall look at instances in which the Council has sought to promote redress at the international or the national levels. There have been instances, such as in the case of the Democratic People's Republic of Korea, in which the Council sought to have allegations of the commission of international crimes referred to the International Criminal Court. There have also been instances in which, for example relating to Sri Lanka, Belarus, and the occupied Palestinian territories, the UN High Commissioner for Human

 | DOI:10.1163/9789004504950_010

Rights, at the request of the Council, has been requested, and has sought to promote redress. We begin with principles of redress.

2 Principles of Redress

In 2006, the UN General Assembly, based on a draft by the former Commission on Human Rights, adopted a set of basic principles and guidelines on the right to remedy and reparation for victims of violations of international human rights law and international humanitarian law.[8] The groundwork for these principles had been done by Professor Theo van Boven in his capacity as Special Rapporteur of the then Sub-Commission on the Prevention of Discrimination and Protection of Minorities.

The basic principles and guidelines contain 13 chapters with core provisions of international human rights law. It calls upon Governments to provide equal and effective access to justice for those who claim to be victims of a human rights or humanitarian law violation, irrespective of who may ultimately be the bearer of responsibility for the violation; and to provide effective remedies to victims, including reparation

The principles underline that States must investigate violations of international human rights law and international humanitarian law. Further, if there is sufficient evidence, they must also submit the person allegedly responsible for the violations to prosecution and, if found guilty, punish her or him. Moreover, in these cases, states should, in accordance with international law, cooperate with one another and assist international judicial organs in these violations.

Victims should be treated with humanity and respect for their dignity and human rights, and appropriate measures should be taken to ensure their safety, physical, and psychological well-being and privacy, as well as that of their families. The state should ensure that its domestic laws provide that a victim who has suffered violence or trauma should benefit from special consideration and care to avoid re-traumatization during legal and administrative procedures.

As remedies for gross violations of rights, the principles include the victim's right to equal and effective access to justice; adequate, effective, and prompt reparation for harm suffered; and access to relevant information concerning violations and reparation mechanisms.

According to the principles, victims of gross violations should have equal access to an effective judicial remedy as provided for under international law.

8 GA resolution 60/147

Other remedies include access to administrative and other bodies, as well as mechanisms, modalities, and proceedings conducted in accordance with domestic law. Obligations arising under international law to secure the right to access justice and fair and impartial proceedings shall be reflected in domestic laws.

In addition to individual access to justice, states should endeavour to develop procedures to allow groups of victims to present claims for reparation and receive reparation. An adequate, effective, and prompt remedy for gross violations of international human rights law or serious violations of international humanitarian law should include all available and appropriate international processes in which a person may have legal standing and should be without prejudice to any other domestic remedies

The principles stipulate that adequate, effective, and prompt reparation is intended to promote justice by redressing gross and serious violations of international human rights law or international humanitarian law. Reparation should be proportional to the gravity of violations and the harm suffered. In accordance with its domestic laws and international legal obligations, a state shall provide reparation to victims for acts or omissions that can be attributed to the state and constitute gross and serious violations of international human rights law or humanitarian law. In cases where a person, a legal person, or other entity is liable for reparation to a victim, such party should provide reparation to the victim or compensate the state if the state has already provided reparation to the victim.

States should endeavor to establish national programs for reparation and other assistance to victims if the party liable for the harm suffered is unable or unwilling to meet their obligations. States should also enforce domestic judgments for reparation against individuals or entities liable for the harm suffered and endeavor to enforce valid foreign legal judgments for reparation in accordance with domestic law and international legal obligations. To that end, states should provide effective mechanisms to enforce reparation judgments under their domestic laws.

Restitution should, whenever possible, restore the victim to the original situation before the violation occurred. Restitution includes, as appropriate: restoration of liberty, enjoyment of human rights, identity, family life and citizenship, return to one's place of residence, restoration of employment, and return of property.

Compensation should be provided for any economically assessable damage resulting from gross and serious violations of international human rights law and international humanitarian law, such as physical or mental harm; lost opportunities, including employment, education, and social benefits; material damages and loss of earnings, including loss of earning potential; moral damage; costs required for legal or expert assistance, medicine and medical services, and psychological and social services.

Rehabilitation should include medical and psychological care as well as legal and social services.

The guidelines further call on states to develop means of informing the general public and, in particular, victims of gross violations of international human rights law and serious violations of international humanitarian law, of the rights and remedies addressed by the principles and of all available legal, medical, psychological, social, administrative, and all other services to which victims may have a right of access. Moreover, victims and their representatives should be entitled to seek and obtain information on the causes leading to their victimization and on the causes and conditions pertaining to the gross and serious violations of international human rights law and international humanitarian law, and to learn the truth about these violations.

The guidelines underline that the application and interpretation of its provisions must be consistent with international human rights law and international humanitarian law, and be without discrimination.

3 Right to Truth

The Human Rights Council is on record as supporting the right to truth. In resolution No 11, on the right to truth, adopted at its ninth session, the Human Rights Council recognized the importance of respecting and ensuring the right to the truth so as to contribute to ending impunity and to promote and protect human rights. It encouraged States to consider establishing specific judicial mechanisms and, where appropriate, truth and reconciliation commissions to complement the justice system, to investigate and address gross violations of human rights and serious violations of international humanitarian law. The Council has a special rapporteur on the right to truth and has adopted normative pronouncements on this issue that we refer to in the chapter below on 'jurisprudence'.

4 Expressions of Concern Over, or Condemnation of Gross Violations

The Human Rights Council has continued the practice of its predecessor, the Commission on Human Rights, in publicly debating situations involving alleged gross violations of human rights, expressing concern over selected situations, condemning gross violations in some instances, and extending technical assistance intended to help Governments overcome difficulties being experienced. It needs to be borne in mind, for a start, that the Council has a number of on-going thematic investigations, conducted by its 'Special Procedures' mandate holders on topics such as arbitrary and extra-judicial executions, torture, enforced and involuntary disappearances, violence against women, trafficking in human beings, arbitrary detention, and a host of other topics. The mandate-holders present annual reports to the Council with their analyses and findings, as well as country-specific reports on countries they have visited.

The reports of the Council's Special Procedures often detail gross violations of human rights across the world and are discussed openly in the Council. The Council regularly adopts resolutions on these topics expressing its concern and making recommendations to Governments. At its forty-fifth session, in October, 2020, for example, In a resolution adopted without a vote on the global environmental situation as it impacted on the rights of the child, the Council urged States to take effective measures to ensure that all children in vulnerable situations can exercise their rights on an equal basis with other children, and that the effects of environmental harm do not affect them disproportionately, including by strengthening the collection of disaggregated data, by requiring that childhood exposure monitoring and children's rights impact assessment procedures take fully into account the impact of proposed policies, programmes and projects on those in the most vulnerable situations, including their gender dimensions, and by providing children at particular risk and their parents, or primary caregivers and legal guardians, with assistance in accessing effective remedies.

At the same forty-fifth regular session, held in October, 2020, the Council adopted resolutions on the situations in Belarus, Venezuela, Syria, Yemen and the Philippines. The Council also discussed and renewed the mandates of its special procedures on the situation in Burundi [a Commission of Inquiry], Venezuela [an Independent international fact-finding mission], Somalia [an Independent Expert], the Situation in Kasai [an International Experts] and the situation of human rights in the Central African Republic [an Independent Expert].

At its 46th session, in March, 2021, the Council pronounced on the COVID-19 pandemic then ravaging the world. In a first resolution on the topic, on ensuring equitable, affordable, timely and universal access for all countries to vaccines in response to the coronavirus disease (COVID-19),adopted without a vote, the Council called upon States and other relevant stakeholders to take appropriate measures to guarantee the fair, transparent, equitable, efficient, universal and timely access and distribution of safe, quality, efficacious, effective, accessible and affordable COVID-19 vaccines and to enable international cooperation on the issue.

In a second resolution on the topic, the Council urged States to immediately take steps to prevent, within their respective legal frameworks, speculation and undue export controls and stockpiling that might hinder affordable timely, equitable and universal access for all countries to COVID-19 vaccines. It strongly urged all States to refrain from taking any economic, financial or trade measures that might adversely affect equitable affordable, fair, timely and universal access to COVID-19 vaccines, in particular in developing countries. The Council also decided to hold, at its forty-ninth session, a panel discussion on the matter.

The Council recognized that developing countries required massive liquidity and financing support to deal with the immediate fall-out from the COVID-19 pandemic and its repercussions for the economy and for all human rights owing to the challenges faced in the areas of healthcare, education, employment and social protection systems, as well as to the heavy debt burden and deteriorating economic buffer.

Also at its 46th session, the Council adopted resolutions on the situation of human rights in Belarus, Cambodia, the Democratic People's Republic of Korea, Georgia, the Islamic Republic of Iran, Mali, Myanmar, Nicaragua, Occupied Palestinian Territory, the Syrian Arab Republic, South Sudan, and Sri Lanka.

We take up the resolutions on Belarus, Sri Lanka, the Democratic People's Republic of Korea and Occupied Palestinian Territory in the section on accountability below. In a resolution on "torture and other cruel, inhuman or degrading treatment or punishment: the roles and responsibilities of police and other law enforcement officials, adopted without a vote, the Council called upon all States to take effective measures to ensure that the use of force by police and other law enforcement officials, including the use of less-lethal weapons, is in conformity with international obligations and the principles of legality, necessity, proportionality, accountability and non-discrimination, and that those using force account for each use of force, bearing in mind that legal force may only be used to protect against grievous bodily harm or an imminent threat to life..

In a resolution on the situation human rights in the Islamic Republic of Iran, adopted by a vote of 21 in favour, 12 against, and 14 abstentions, the Council extended the mandate of its Special Rapporteur on Iran and called upon the Government to cooperate fully with the Special Rapporteur and to permit access to visit the country and to provide all information necessary to allow the fulfilment of the mandate.

In a resolution on the situation of human rights in Myanmar, adopted without a vote, the Council extended the mandate of its Special Rapporteur on the situation and invited the Special Rapporteur to continue to monitor the situation of human rights and to measure progress in the implementation of recommendations. Just prior to its 46th regular session, the Council had held a special session the situation in Myanmar and had adopted a resolution condemning gross violations of human rights underway.

5 Accountability

The Human Rights Council has a limited practice of pursuing accountability for gross violations of human rights. At its 46th session, in 2021, for example, the Council adopted a resolution on promoting reconciliation, accountability and human rights in Sri Lanka, adopted by a vote of 22 in favour, 11 against and 14 abstentions in which it requested the Office of High Commissioner to enhance its monitoring and reporting on the situation of human rights in Sri Lanka, including on progress in reconciliation and accountability. The Council decided to strengthen the capacity of the Office of the High Commissioner to collect, consolidate, analyse and preserve information and evidence and to develop possible strategies for future accountability processes for gross violations of human rights or serious violations of international humanitarian law in Sri Lanka, to advocate for victims and survivors, and to support relevant judicial and other proceedings, including in Member States with competent jurisdiction.

In a second resolution adopted at the 46th session, on the situation of human rights in Belarus in the run-up to the 2020 Presidential election and its aftermath, adopted by a vote of 20 in favour, 7 against and 20 abstentions, the Council requested the High Commissioner, with assistance from relevant experts and special procedure mandate holders, inter alia, to monitor and report on the situation of human rights, to carry out a comprehensive examination of all alleged human rights violations committed in Belarus since 1 May,2020, including the possible gender dimensions of such violations, to establish the facts and circumstances surrounding the alleged violations, and to collect, consolidate, preserve and analyse information and evidence with a view to contributing to accountability for perpetrators and justice for victims and, where possible, to identify those responsible.[9]

9 On 24 March, 2021 a group of Nineteen states adopted a Joint Statement in support of the establishment of an International Accountability Platform for Belarus. The statement

In a third resolution adopted at the 46th session, on the situation of human rights in the Democratic People's Republic of Korea, adopted without a vote, the Council decided to continue to strengthen, for a period of two years, the capacity of the Office of the High Commissioner for Human Rights, including its field-based structure in Seoul, to allow the implementation of relevant recommendations made by the group of independent experts on accountability in its report aimed at strengthening current monitoring and documentation efforts, establishing a central information and evidence repository and having experts in legal accountability assess all information and testimonies with a view to developing possible strategies to be used in any future accountability process. The Council also decided to extend for one year the mandate of its Special Rapporteur on human rights in the Democratic People's Republic of Korea.

In a fourth resolution adopted at the 46th session, on the human rights situation in the Occupied Palestinian Territory, including East Jerusalem, and the obligation to ensure accountability and justice, adopted by a vote of 32 in favour, 6 against, and 8 abstentions, the Council called on Israel, the occupying Power, to comply immediately with its international law obligations to the protected occupied population, and ensure non-discriminatory access to vaccines for immunization against the coronavirus disease (COVID-19) in the Occupied Palestinian Territory, including East Jerusalem, including in coordination with the Government of the State of Palestine.

At the end of the day, it is a matter of elementary justice that gross violations of human rights be recorded, that efforts be made to bring perpetrators to justice, if possible, and that measures of redress be provided to the victims or their families. The Human Rights Council is a body with a moral mandate but with a membership that is politically driven. Still, in the face of history, the Council should strive to raise its game when it comes to the pursuit of justice

---

declared: "As human rights violations are reoccurring in a culture of impunity in Belarus on a daily basis there is an urgent need to ensure that evidence and documentation are collected and preserved in a secure and appropriate manner in accordance with international standards. The International Accountability Platform for Belarus (IAPB) has taken on the responsibility of the collection, consolidation, verification and preservation of information, documentation and evidence of serious violations of international human rights law committed in Belarus. ...We hereby provide our political support to this urgent action of IAPB. We also reaffirm our support for the establishment of a UN Human Rights Council mandated investigation under the Office of the High Commissioner for Human Rights and supported by relevant experts aimed at contributing to accountability for perpetrators and justice for victims in Belarus."

and redress. The Council is at least on record when it comes to the issue of transitional justice, which we refer to next.

6 Transitional Justice

In resolution No. 10, on transitional justice, adopted without a vote at its ninth session, the Council welcomed the importance and urgency of national and international efforts to restore justice and the rule of law in conflict and post-conflict situations and, where relevant, in the context of transitional processes. It underlined the need for the rights of both victims and accused persons to be respected, in accordance with international standards, with particular attention paid to those most affected by conflicts and the breakdown of the rule of law, among them women, children, migrants, refugees, persons with disabilities and persons belonging to minorities and indigenous peoples, and to ensure that specific measures are taken for their free participation and protection and for the sustainable return of refugees and internally displaced persons in safety and dignity.[10]

7 Evaluation

In the section above on the Council's expressions of concern over, or condemnations of gross violations of human rights, we summarised actions of the Council at its 45th and 46th sessions. In order to provide a sense of perspective on how the Council responded to needy situations world-wide we reproduce next the following parts of a statement issued immediately after the 46th session of the Council by the NGO, International Service on Human Rights:

> *"Human Rights Situations that Merits the HRC's attention*
>
> "The next session will receive a report on pushback from the Special Rapporteur on human rights of migrants. The Council must respond to the severity and scale of *pushbacks and other human rights violations faced by migrants and refugees* in transit and at borders and the ongoing suppression of solidarity, including by answering the High Commissioner's call for independent monitoring. The Council's silence feeds impunity.

10 Resolution 9/10, Human rights and transitional justice, adopted without a vote on 24 September, 2008.

It must build on the momentum of the joint statement of over 90 States reaffirming their commitment to protection of the human rights of migrants regardless of status.

"While the OHCHR expressed deep concern about the deteriorating human rights situation and the ongoing crackdown on civil society in *Algeria*, and called for the immediate and unconditional release of arbitrarily detained individuals, the Council has remained largely silent. As authorities are increasingly arbitrarily and violently arresting protesters – at least 1,500 since the resumption of the Hirak pro-democracy movement on 18 February, we call on the Council to address the criminalisation of public freedoms, to protect peaceful protestors, activists and the media.

Cameroon is one of the human rights crises the Council has failed to address for too long. We condemn the acts of intimidation and reprisal exercised by the Cameroonian government in response to NGOs raising concerns, including Defend Defenders. This is unacceptable behaviour by a Council member. The Council should consider collective action to address the gross human rights violations and abuses occurring in the country.

"We echo the calls of many governments for the Council to step up its meaningful action to ensure that concerns raised by civil society, the UN Special Procedures and the OHCHR about the human rights situation in *China* be properly addressed, including through an independent international investigation. We also regret that a number of States have taken an unprincipled approach of voicing support to actions, such as those by the Chinese government, including in Xinjiang and Hong Kong through their national and other joint statements.

"We call for the Council's attention on the rapid deterioration of human rights in *India*. Violent crackdowns on recent farmers' protests, internet shutdowns in protest areas, sedition and criminal charges against journalists reporting on those protests, and criminalisation of human rights defenders signal an ongoing dangerous trend in restrictions of fundamental freedoms in India. We call on India to ensure fundamental freedoms and allow journalists, HRDs and civil society to continue their legitimate work without intimidation and fear of reprisals.

" We once again regret the lack of Council's attention on the human rights crisis in *Kashmir*. Fundamental freedoms in the Indian-administered Kashmir remains severely curtailed since the revocation of the constitutional autonomy in August 2019. Raids in October and November 2020 on residences and offices of human rights defenders and civil

> society organizations by India's anti-terrorism authorities in a clear attempt of intimidation have further exacerbated the ongoing crisis. We call on OHCHR to continue to monitor and regularly report to the Council on the situation in both Indian and Pakistani administered Kashmir, and on Indian and Pakistani authorities to give the OHCHR and independent observers unfettered access to the region.
>
> "Nearly six months since its adoption, the Council resolution 45/33 on technical assistance to *the Philippines* has proven utterly insufficient to address the widespread human rights violations and persistent impunity. Killings in the war on drugs continue, and attacks on human rights defenders and activists have escalated. The killings of nine unarmed activists on 7 March 2021[11] clearly demonstrates that no amount of technical assistance will end the killings as long as the President and senior officials continue to incite violence and killings as official State policy. It is imperative that the Council sets up an international accountability mechanism to end the cycle of violence and impunity in the Philippines."[12]

The foregoing statement of civil society raises the following questions: first, Cameroon, a serving member of the Council, has allegedly been grossly violating human rights. Second, the Council, for political reasons, frequently resorts to the sham approach of offering technical assistance to Governments grossly violating human rights. One could see the futility of this approach in the case of the Philippines. It is beyond comprehension that the Council did not react to the Government's brazen murder of nine human rights defenders while the Council was actually in session, and openly acknowledged by the President of the Philippines. Third, one could see the political power of China at work. Even more, the civil society statement deprecated "that a number of States have taken an unprincipled approach of voicing support for actions, such as those by the Chinese government, including in Xinjiang and Hong Kong through their national and other joint statements." Fourth, one could also see the political power of India in warding off condemnation of its brazen actions. Fifth, one could see Algeria's political influence at work in shielding it against criticisms for gross violations of human rights. Sixth, one could see the pleas of civil society that 'The Council's silence feeds impunity' in respect of 'push-backs and other human rights violations faced by migrants and refugees in transit and at borders and the ongoing suppression of solidarity'.

---

11 Author's comment: This occurred while the Council was actually in session.

12 "HRC46/Civil Society presents key takeaways from Human Rights Council", issued on 24 March,2021.

8 Conclusion

In this chapter, on redress, we have seen a few significant features in the practice of the Council. First, its thematic special procedures investigate allegations of gross violations of human rights across the world, present findings and analyses to the Council with their recommendations, which are discussed in the Council followed by the adoption of resolutions expressing concern, expressing condemnations, and adopting recommendations for consideration by Governments. This, in our submission, is an inherent process of redress.

Second, although it is admittedly selective because of the inherently political processes operating inside the Council, the world body does take up some country situations in respect of which there are allegations of gross violations of human rights. The Council uses a range of fact-finding actors to look closer into such situations, adopts resolutions expressing concern, condemns gross violations, and thereby expresses the conscience of the international community. Unfortunately, not all situations deserving of such attention receive it. One saw this starkly in the civil society statement deprecating the fact that the Council failed to take actions in respect of egregious violations of human rights in Cameroon, inexplicably a Council member, the Philippines, China, India, and Kashmir. One could also see the politicization of the Council at work in the slender votes by resolutions are adopted. Sometimes resolutions are adopted by narrow margins, or by a minority of the membership of the Council, because the Governments concerned lobby their supporters heavily. For the inhabitants of the countries in respect of which condemnatory resolutions are adopted, they represent a form of redress inasmuch as there is recognition of the injustices taking place inside the country.

Third, the Council has taken a position of principle in favour of the right to truth, and one of its thematic special procedures is devoted to this topic. The Council has also encouraged measures of transitional justice. Both of these items are intended to promote forms of redress.

Fourth, as we saw in relation to the situations in Belarus, the Democratic People's Republic of Korea, Occupied Palestinian Territory, and Sri Lanka, the Council has pushed for accountability and is pioneering a new approach that involves the collection, analysis, and storage of information on alleged gross violations of human rights with a view to their eventual use in trials or other justice procedures nationally, regionally or internationally.

Fifth, while the redress attempted inside the Council is far from perfect, it does represent a limited measure of striving for some measure of justice, to the extent feasible, in the imperfect and heavily politicized and polarized world inevitably reflected in the Council.

CHAPTER 9

Justice

1 Introduction

It would be fair to say that while the Human Rights Council, at its core, is not an organ *of* justice, inasmuch as it applies different weights and measures to different situations, it is an organ *for* justice, inasmuch as it strives to help relieve the plight of the poor, and to act for the promotion and protection of the rights of minorities, indigenous populations, Afro-descendants and other groups of people in distress. In the preceding chapter we already made the point that the prevailing mantra in the Council, even when dealing with situations of gross violations of human rights, is to engage in dialogue and cooperation, which can mean that the Council is often not forthright in condemning gross violations of human rights and does, indeed, do so selectively.

In this chapter, instead of looking at the Human Rights Council as an organ *of* justice, we shall look, rather, at the work of the Council *for* justice. We shall take as examples the work of the Council to help alleviate the plight of the extremely poor, and other groups in distress. Before looking at these specific instances, we shall first discuss, for background, the idea of justice as it featured in the discussions leading to the adoption of the International Bill of Human Rights. In an ideal world, the idea of justice in the International Bill of Rights should guide the UN Human Rights Council throughout its work.

To set our subject matter in perspective, we discuss, first, a phenomenon that, without a doubt, marks out the Human Rights Council, namely the undemocratic character of many of the Governments sitting on it as Members or as Observers. There can be no doubt that this is a defining characteristic of the Council, one that is not likely to go away any time soon. The 2021 Global Trends report put out by the Strategic Futures Group of the US National Intelligence Council makes the following assessment:

> A key consequence of greater imbalance [in the world] is greater contestation within communities, states, and the international community. This encompasses rising tensions, division, and competition in societies, states, and at the international level. Many societies are increasingly divided among identity affiliations and at risk of greater fracturing. Relationships between societies and governments will be under persistent strain as states struggle to meet rising demands from populations.

 | DOI:10.1163/9789004504950_011

> As a result, politics within states are likely to grow more volatile and contentions, and no region, ideology, or governance system seems immune or to have the answers. At the international level, the geopolitical environment will be more competitive – shaped by China's challenge to the United States and Western-led international system. Major powers are jockeying to establish and exploit new rules of the road. This contestation is playing out across domains from information and the media to trade and technological innovations.[1]

In this setting democracy is, and is likely to be, under increasing stress world-wide.

2 The Decline of Democracy in the World

Freedom in the World, the 2021 annual report of Freedom House, a US government-sponsored institution, carried the title, *Democracy Under Siege*.[2] The report noted with sadness that 2021 marked the 15th consecutive year of decline in global freedom. In 2020, 82 countries were free, 59 partly free, and 54 not free. The countries experiencing deterioration outnumbered those with improvements by the largest margin recorded since the negative trend began in 2006. Whereas, in 2005, thirty-one countries had made positive advances, in 2020 forty-five countries had regressed. The proportion of 'Not Free' countries had reached the highest it had been in the past fifteen years.

Over the previous year, the report continued, oppressive and often violent authoritarian forces had tipped the international order in their favour time and again, exploiting both the advantages of non-democratic systems and the weaknesses in ailing democracies. In a variety of environments, flickers of hope were extinguished, contributing to a new global *status quo* in which acts of repression went unpunished and democracy's advocates were increasingly isolated.

Democracy's defenders, the report continued, had sustained heavy new losses in their struggle against authoritarian foes, shifting the international balance in favour of tyranny. Incumbent leaders increasingly used force to crush opponents and settle scores, sometimes in the name of public health [the COVID-19 pandemic], while beleaguered activists – lacking effective

1 The Strategic Futures Group of the US National Intelligence Group, Global Trends, March 2021: Key Themes, p. 3: https://www.dni.gov/index.php/gt2040-home/keythemes.

2 Freedom House, Freedom Report 2021: Democracy Under Siege. Washington D.C., 2021.

international support – faced heavy jail sentences, torture or murder in many settings.[3]

The impact of the long-term democratic decline had become increasingly global in nature, broad enough to be felt by those living under the cruelest dictatorships, as well as by citizens of long-standing democracies. Nearly 75 percent of the world's population lived in a country that faced deterioration in 2020. The ongoing decline had given rise to claims of democracy's inherent inferiority. Proponents of this idea included official Chinese and Russian commentators seeking to strengthen their international influence while escaping accountability for abuses, as well as anti-democratic actors within democratic states who saw an opportunity to consolidate power. They were both cheering the breakdown of democracy and exacerbating it, pitting themselves against the brave groups and individuals who had set out to reverse the damage.

The parlous state of US democracy had been conspicuous in the early days of 2021 as an insurrectionist mob, egged on by the words of outgoing president Donald Trump and his refusal to admit defeat in the November 2020 election, stormed the US Capitol building and temporarily disrupted Congress's final certification of the vote. This capped a year in which the Trump administration had attempted to undermine accountability for malfeasance, including by dismissing inspectors-general responsible for rooting out financial and other misconduct in government; amplified false allegations of electoral fraud that had fed mistrust among much of the US population; and condoned disproportionate violence by police in response to massive protests calling for an end to systemic racial injustice.

> But the outburst of political violence at the symbolic heart of US democracy, incited by the president himself, threw the country into even greater crisis. Notwithstanding the inauguration of a new president in keeping with the law and the constitution, the United States will need to work vigorously to strengthen its institutional safeguards, restore its civic norms, and uphold the promise of its core principles for all segments of society if it is to protect its venerable democracy and regain global credibility.[4]

India's status, the Freedom House report continued, had declined from Free to Partly Free due to a multi-year pattern in which the Hindu nationalist government and its allies had presided over rising violence and discriminatory

3 As this book is being written, the Military in Myanmar (Burma) had overturned the results of democratic elections and was shooting down innocent demonstrators by the hundreds.

4 Ibid., p. 4.

practices affecting the Muslim population and pursued a crackdown on expressions of dissent by the media, academics, civil society groups and protesters.

In an Editorial of 6 March, 2021commenting on the report, the Financial Times expressed sadness that democracy was in retreat and that three quarters of the global population in 2020 lived in countries where freedom was falling, while less than twenty percent lived in a free country. The shifting global balance reflected not just a decline of democracies but a fightback by autocracies. The Financial Times commented:

> Democracy promotion must begin at home. The US and its allies must repair their own political systems so they can again lead by example. That means strengthening institutions, making electoral systems fair and protecting them from interference. As Freedom House notes, it also means addressing the root causes of dissatisfaction … Western democracies … should step up support and solidarity to rights groups and democracy activists, by imposing sanctions or cutting business ties or aid to governments engaged in crackdowns.[5]

Janan Ganesh, writing in the Financial Times on 10 March 2021, observed: "Were it not for Israel, a … motorist could drive from Russia's north-eastern, Alaska-facing tip to the south-western point of Angola without passing through a 'free' or even 'partly free' country. That daunting map alone earned *Democracy Under Siege*, the report by the Freedom House watchdog, its lurid title."[6] The article highlighted the following sobering facts about the decline of democracy in the world:

- In no year since 2005 have more countries improved their democratic institutions than weakened them.
- Recent malefactors include the strongest nation, the US,[7] and the second most populous, India.
- China, the potential master of the century, scored nine out of 100 for overall freedom.

Ganesh commented: "… [I]f the West could not entrench freedom as the global standard when it was ascendant, it is hardly likely to as the balance of world power tilts increasingly eastward."[8]

---

5 Financial Times, "Democracy promotion must begin at home", Editorial, 6 March, 2021.

6 Janan Ganesh, "The decline of democracy is not America's responsibility", Financial Times, 10 March, 2021, p. 19.

7 Note by the author of this book: Under the Presidency of Donald Trump.

8 Loc. Cit.

The decline of democracy in the world impacts directly on the quality of the commitment to justice, or lack thereof, of the Members of the Human Rights Council. Alas, we also see, world-wide a decline of human rights justice in the world.

3 The Decline of Human Rights Justice in the World

In addition to the democratic decline discussed in the previous section, there is a parallel decline of human rights justice in the world. Indeed, the soul of the UN and its Universal Declaration of Human Rights is being destroyed with the disappearance of human rights justice in the world.

International law requires that Governments comply with their obligations, be they obligations of conduct or of result. The oldest supervisory body in the UN system, the ILO Committee on the Application of Standards, going back to 1919, laid down the standard, initially followed by UN human rights treaty bodies, that regardless of the political, economic, social, cultural, legal, or philosophical complexion of a country, it must comply with its international human rights obligations. Justice should be the yardstick.

But no more, at the United Nations. Its Human Rights Council prioritizes dialogue and cooperation over 'confrontation', namely the principled denunciation of violations. A devastating UN report on crimes against humanity in North Korea met with no referral to the International Criminal Court. Justice did not matter.

China and Russia have moved resolutions in the General Assembly and the Human Rights Council that prioritize dialogue over justice. The General Assembly, as a result, has called upon the human rights treaty monitoring organs to give preference to dialogue and cooperation. The Human Rights Council, for its part, called for attention to 'traditional values' instead of implementation of the letter of international human rights law.

The United States of America has a long-standing practice of only occasionally submitting to the supervision of human rights treaty bodies. The USA, like China, India and Russia, does not accept the jurisdiction of the International Criminal Court. US troops abroad may commit all manner of atrocities but are only amenable, if at all, to US justice.

In the United Kingdom there are those in the ruling Conservative party who rail against the jurisdiction of the European Court of Justice and press for the country to withdraw from the jurisdiction of the European Court of Human Rights. Domestic institutions are preferred to regional ones even though the latter comprise multiple judges, highly qualified, from European countries.

Churchill had led the establishment of the Council of Europe and its human rights machinery, but that does not count these days.

Russia implements few decisions of the European Court of Human Rights, threatening all the time to withdraw from the European Convention of Human Rights. The Inter-American Court of Human Rights has been a splendid organ of justice but many Member States of the OAS have found this uncomfortable and have either withdrawn from its jurisdiction or are threatening to do so. The body is in existential crisis.

In Africa, it took a long time for the African Commission on Human and Peoples' Rights to grow some teeth, but it is a matter of luck and chance whether its decisions are implemented by the countries concerned. The African Court of Human Rights is a more recent body and so its experience so far has been limited.

There is no pan-Asian human rights body. There is an ASEAN Human Rights Commission but its remit is diplomacy, rather than justice. The two major Asian powers, China and India, are both practitioners of realpolitik when it comes to the international enforcement of human rights. China nominally professes adherence to the universality of human rights but, in reality, the ruling Party decides on its own values and does whatever it wishes. Its writ is rule by law, not the rule of law. No human rights justice here.

China's Belt and Road Initiative is oblivious to human rights concerns. It provided assistance to countries, such as Zimbabwe under former President Robert Mugabe, regardless of their human rights records. It openly downplays international human rights norms.

India also professes adherence to the universality of human rights and its judiciary has a respectable record of applying the rule of law within the country. But Indian troops in contested areas may carry out atrocities at will, without domestic or international scrutiny. No justice here.

UN High Commissioners for Human Rights and UN Secretaries-General do sometimes give voice to human rights concerns and plead for justice. But the structure of the international system is such that, often, their voices do not carry far. And there are few instances of reparation or compensation for the victims of violations of human rights.

The International Court of Justice has in the past laid down some laudable principles of justice. But few countries would accept its jurisdiction on human rights issues. It is instructive to see the published views articulated by the current Chinese judge on the World Court:

- First. China is of the view that the human rights cause should be promoted in line with each State's social and economic development. China believes that as a social movement, human rights promotion should proceed in a gradual and incremental fashion. In principle, human right protection remains in relative terms for every country, subject to the level and degree of its development.

- Second, while accepting universality and inseparability of human rights, China attaches importance to economic, social and cultural rights and the right to development in its human rights process. It shares the view that the essential task for most developed countries at this stage is first and foremost to pursue economic and social development. China accords precedence of economic and social rights over civil and political rights.
- Third, China also emphasizes the correlation between the human rights cause and the rule of law. In promoting rights and freedoms China lays stress on duties and obligations of citizens under the rule of law.
- Fourth, in promoting international protection of human rights, China advocates mutual respect, non-interference, non-confrontational and constructive dialogues. It opposes "the double standards practised against the developing world".

This statement of the Chinese position speaks for itself. Essentially, it represents the approach of the majority of UN Member States.

What place, then, for justice for the victims of violations. The decline of human rights justice in the world is palpable. The question deserves to be asked, who will stand up for justice for humanity in these circumstances? Young people the world over continue to agitate for justice, as could be seen when the Military in Myanmar (Burma) overthrew the results of free elections by force and proceeded to shoot down by the hundreds innocent young people demonstrating for the restoration of democracy.

The human rights vision launched by the United Nations in 1947 embraced an International Bill of Rights with a Universal Declaration, binding treaties, and measures of implementation. Even in those difficult, Cold War times, justice was the leading idea that animated the drafters of the Universal Declaration, as we shall see next.

4 The Idea of Justice in Philosophical Literature

The idea of justice is much discussed in the philosophical literature from Socrates and Plato to our times, with leading contemporary contributions from John Rawls, Michael Sandel and Amartya Sen. Aristotle considered justice the pre-eminent virtue, as did Mortimer Adler, the late editor of the Encyclopedia Britannica. One could say that justice should inspire the quest for the articulation and implementation of rights and that the normative content and application of human rights should meet the requirements of justice. As we shall see below, Amartya Sen, in his recent work on the Idea of Justice offers, in its 17th chapter, offered a theory of human rights that is somewhat removed from international practice and jurisprudence – which raises the question of who determines what rights are: philosophers or consensual decisions of the international community. Indeed, philosophical writings apart, one could argue that ethical principles are consensual, negotiated, legislated, adjudicated, and nurtured.

In this section, we shall discuss the idea of justice as it may be distilled from the International Bill of Human Rights, which consists of the Universal Declaration of Human Rights of 1948, the International Covenant on Economic, Social and Cultural Rights, and the International Covenant on Civil and Political Rights, both of 1966. These instruments bring out elements of justice according to which:

- Society, somewhat as envisaged by Plato, shall be organized for justice (Article 28 of the Universal Declaration)
- All human beings are born free and equal indignity and rights (Article 1 of the Universal Declaration), recalling Aristotle's reasoning that justice is some form of equality.
- Everyone shall be granted equality before the law and shall be entitled to due process of law.
- Everyone should be provided with equal opportunity for a decent life
- Government should strive to prevent violations of human rights and provide remedies and compensation where they have been breached.
- Justice shall be provided for the disadvantaged
- The principle of justice underlies international human rights norms. Everyone shall be treated humanely and inhuman acts shall be prohibited.
- The principle of justice is reinforced by the principle of equity.

Before developing these submissions it would be appropriate to provide, by way of background, a brief outline of the leading philosophical views on the idea of justice. In the discussion that follows we draw upon Curtis's leading work, The Great Political Theories.[9] Justice, according to Socrates, is good in itself and not for its consequences. Plato's Republic argues that justice pays apart from its consequences. One of the fundamental ideas that Plato put forward in his defence of justice was that we should look for a general theory of goodness.

9 Michael Curtis, The Great Political Theories. Vols. I and II. New York, Avon Books, 1961.

Aristotle considered that the good in the sphere of politics is justice; and justice consisted in what tends to promote the common interest. General opinion makes it consist in some form of equality . Justice involves two factors – things, and the persons to whom things are assigned – and it considers that persons who are equal should have assigned to them equal things. But here a question arises which must not be overlooked. Equals and unequals – yes; but equals and unequals *in what?* This is a question that raises difficulties and involves us in philosophical speculation on politics. It is possible to argue that offices and honours ought to be distributed unequally on the basis of superiority *in any respect whatsoever* – even though there were similarity, and no shadow of any difference, in every other respect; and it may be urged in favour of this argument that where people differ from one another there must be a difference in what is just and proportionate to their merits. If this argument were accepted, the mere fact of a better complexion, or greater height, or any other such advantage, would establish a claim for a greater share of political rights to be given to its possessor.

Cicero was of the view that since all men have received reason, therefore all men have received Justice, for justice is one, it binds all human society, and is based on one Law, which is right reason. Whoever knows not this Law, whether it has been recorded in writing anywhere or not, is without Justice. But if Justice is conformity to written laws and national customs, and if everything is to be tested by the standard of utility, then anyone who thinks it will be profitable to him will, if he is able, disregard and violate the laws. It follows that Justice does not exist at all, if it does not exist in nature, and if that form of it which is based on utility can be overthrown by that very utility itself.

And if nature is not to be considered the foundation of Justice, that will mean the destruction of the virtues on which human society depends. For where then will there be a place for generosity, or love of country, or loyalty, or the inclination to be of service to others or to show gratitude for favours received? For these virtues originate in our natural inclination to love our fellowmen, and this is the foundation of Justice. "Otherwise not merely consideration for men but also rites and pious observances in honour of the gods are done away with; for I think that these ought to be maintained, not through fear, but on account of the close relationship which exists between man and God."[10]

St Augustine considered that true justice has no existence save in that republic whose founder and ruler is Christ. Augustine cites Cicero in De Republica: He notes the people, according to Cicero, is an assemblage

10 Cicero, On the Commonwealth, Book III, xi and xii.

associated by a common acknowledgement of right and by a community of interests. And what Cicero meant by a common acknowledgement of right was that a republic cannot be administered without justice. For that which is done by right is justly done, and what is unjustly done cannot be done by right: for justice is that virtue which gives everyone his due.

Immanuel Kant was concerned with the moral law and the autonomy of will. He considered freedom as being autonomy. Laws were those conditions under which the will of one individual could be united with those of others according to a general law of freedom. In obeying the moral law, man was obeying an internal law, the result of his reason. Man should act because he is aware that he ought to act. The principle of all morality was self-determination. But man should act on the basis of the "categorical imperative": "Act according to that maxim which you can at the same time will to be a universal law." One should act on the basis of general principles which were intuitively recognized and not self-contradictory, such as the keeping of promises or telling the truth.

Every action, according to Kant, must be in accordance with Right, which enables the freedom of each man's will to exist together with the freedom of all others according to the universal law. All persons should be treated as ends; "Treat humanity, in your own person, and in the person of everyone else, always as an end as well as a means, never merely as a means." Here Kant was influenced by Rousseau's idea of the dignity of man. Kant thus stressed the rights of man, equality before the law, the need for correct legal procedures and an educational process that would increase enlightenment. Internationally, he pleaded, as did Rousseau, for a system of world peace and for world citizenship. Optimistically, he believed that the guarantee of perpetual peace was given by nature which showed a design to make harmony spring from human discord.

John Stuart Mill argued for a fundamental principle that men, acting in their own self-interest, sought pleasure and avoided pain, the two qualities which determined behaviour. Pleasure alone was regarded as good, pain was seen as evil. The utility of everything, therefore, depended on its contribution to the first and the avoidance of the latter. Government, acting according to the principle of utility, sought to increase pleasure and decrease pain, and thus attain the greatest happiness of the greatest number.

Mill specifically discussed the relationship between utility and justice. He considered that the best grounding we can give to our intuitions of justice is in the end a utilitarian one. Mill wrote that while our sense of justice comes from a primitive pair of instincts (self-defence and sympathy), its content has a utilitarian basis.

The objection to Mill comes from our sense that justice has a special kind of binding force on us and leads to moral assessments which are quite different from those we would expect a utilitarian to make. Mill says that people find it difficult to see in justice only a particular kind or branch of general utility and thinking that its superior binding force requires a totally different origin. The jury is out on the question of whether utility is consistent with justice, let alone whether it offers the best formulation of it. Can utility, acting so as to increase the sum of human happiness, be something we can achieve by acting against our sense of what is just (e.g. a judge knowingly sentencing someone for a crime he did not commit because the judge thinks it would deter crimes)?

John Rawls considered that justice is about treating people fairly. At the heart of his work was the idea that we need to think clearly about how we live together and the ways in which the state influences our lives. For our existence to be tolerable we need to cooperate. Rawls developed a theory of justice based on two principles he thought all reasonable people would accept: the principles of freedom and equality. The first principle was his Liberty Principle, which states that everyone should have the right to a range of basic freedoms that must not be taken away from them, such as freedom of belief, freedom to vote for their leaders, and extensive freedom of expression. Rawls' second principle, the difference principle, is about equality. Society should be arranged to give more equal wealth and opportunity to the most disadvantaged. Rawls, followed by Michael Sandel, Thomas Pogge, Martha Nussbaum and Will Kymlicka, all believed that philosophy should engage with the deep and difficult questions about how we can and should live together. They believed that philosophy should actually change how we live, not just change how to discuss how we live.

Michael Sandel, in his book on Justice, notes that three ideas point to a different way of thinking about justice: maximizing welfare, respecting freedom, and promoting virtue. Amartya Sen, in his book on justice, offers a theory of human rights according to which human rights are moral rights that protect important freedoms and entail social obligations that people promote these freedoms. Human rights are moral rights "really strong ethical pronouncements as to what should be done . They are not legal rights, though they are often enshrined in legal documents and institutions. Second, the purpose of human rights is to protect important freedoms. Sen's analysis of freedom includes an "opportunity aspect". But human rights go beyond the capabilities approach in protecting the process according to which [they] receive these functionings. Third, human rights do not protect all freedoms. Rather, they must meet "threshold conditions" of sufficient social importance to be included as part of the human rights of the person and correspondingly to generate obligations for others to see how they can help the person to realize those freedoms" Fourth, human rights entail social obligations .

Having presented a skeletal summary of philosophical writings on the idea of justice, we now proceed to discuss the idea of justice in the International Bill of Rights.

5 The Idea of Justice in the International Bill of Human Rights

In this section we return here, for context, to the idea of justice in the International Bill of Human Rights which was treated in an earlier chapter of this book. The Universal Declaration of Human Rights states that recognition of the inherent dignity and of the equal and inalienable rights of all members of the human family is the *foundation of freedom, justice and peace in the world.* It is essential, if man is not to be compelled to have recourse, as a last resort, to rebellion against tyranny and oppression, that human rights should be protected by the rule of law. The International Covenant on Civil and Political Rights recognizes that the rights it contains are derived from the inherent dignity of the human person. The ideal of free human beings enjoying civil and political rights and freedom from fear and want. Women and men are entitled to equal rights.

All human beings, the Universal Declaration affirms, are born free and equal in dignity and rights. Everyone has the right to life, liberty and security of person. (3) No one shall be subjected to slavery or servitude (4). No one shall be subjected to torture (5). Everyone has the right to recognition everywhere as a person before the law (5) Everyone is equal before the law and is entitled to equal protection of the law (7). Everyone has the right to an effective remedy (8). No one should be subjected to arbitrary arrest or detention or exile (9). Everyone is entitled to a fair and public hearing by an independent and impartial tribunal (10). Everyone is to be presumed innocent (11). Everyone has the right to freedom of thought, conscience and religion (18). Everyone has the right to freedom of opinion and expression (19). The will of the people shall be the basis of the authority of government (21). Everyone is entitled to social security. The International Covenant on Economic, Social and Cultural Rights elaborates on this and related rights. Everyone is entitled to a social and international order in which the rights in the Universal Declaration can be realized.

Articles 1 and 2 of the Universal Declaration, building on the human rights provisions of the UN Charter, laid the foundations of the contemporary international legal order and are of the greatest importance legally, philosophically, and from the perspectives of international public policy. Even though the Universal Declaration, as such, was professedly considered a moral rather than a legal document, Articles 1 and 2 had implicit legal status and made 'instant international customary law' because of the 'higher value' of the self-evident truths contained in Article 1, the fact that the non-discrimination provisions in Article 2 reiterated and expanded on the Charter's non-discrimination legal obligations, and because of the consensus that flowed into these articles.

The General Assembly was effectively announcing to the world that the future governance of humanity must be on the basis of the principles contained in these two articles. This point can be made in another way: is it conceivable that the world could be governed on any other basis than that provided in Articles 1 and 2?

The clarity and force of the provisions of Articles 1 and 2 bear out their historic legal. philosophical, and policy significance.: All human beings, Article 1 proclaimed, are born free and equal in dignity and rights. They are endowed with reason and conscience and should act towards one another in a spirit of brotherhood. Everyone, Article 2 declared, is entitled to all the rights and freedoms set forth in the Declaration without distinction of any kind such as race, colour, sex, language, religion, political or other opinion, national or social origin, property, birth or other status. Furthermore, no distinction shall be made on the basis of the political, jurisdictional or international status of the country or territory to which a person belongs, whether it be independent, trust, non-self-governing or under any other limitation of sovereignty. In tracing the drafting of Article 2, Morsink highlighted three points: the article reiterated the Charter's non-discrimination principle; the prohibited grounds of discrimination were expanded; and a strong effort was made to extend the principles of equality and non-discrimination to the peoples of non-self-governing territories.

The normative obligations of Governments henceforth would be to:

- To recognize in their constitutional, legal and governance systems the freedom, dignity, equality and fundamental human rights of every person on the planet.
- To legislate for, and uphold, the principle of equality and non-discrimination for every human being.
- To recognize and apply the foregoing normative precepts to the inhabitants of non-self-governing territories.
- To govern on the basis of the principles of international solidarity and cooperation.

On the philosophical significance of the provisions of Articles 1 and 2, UNESCO, as a contribution to the drafting of the Declaration, had approached a group of philosophers to help think through the philosophical aspects of a future declaration. The UNESCO group concluded that it was not possible to achieve agreement across cultures concerning certain rights that 'may be seen as implicit in man's nature as an individual and as a member of society and to follow from the fundamental right to live.'

At the first meeting of the drafting committee of the Commission on Human Rights, when it considered the initial draft prepared by John Humphrey and his staff in the Secretariat, Col. Hodgson (Australia) asked "what was the 'philosophy' behind the paper? What principles did they adopt; what method did they follow? Is it their own idea; is it a collection of various principles". Humphrey replied that he could not oblige Colonel Hodgson "for the simple reason that [the draft] is based on no philosophy whatsoever." He had been asked to compile a list of rights for discussion purposes, and that was what he had done.[11]

During the drafting of the Universal Declaration, the Chinese representative, P.C. Chang, commented that Article 1 rested on the basis of eighteenth century philosophy. That philosophy was based on the innate goodness of man.[12] In declaring human rights for human beings the drafters sought to protect everyone with human attributes: a thinking being capable of consciousness (experience of thoughts and sensations), with memory, beliefs, hopes and emotions, able to perform actions, which makes them moral agents responsible for what they do.[13] The drafters were reacting against the Holocaust, grounded in theories of racial superiority, of superior and inferior human beings, and of a genocidal campaign against the latter. Protection of peoples from genocide had featured in resolution 96(I) adopted a year before the Universal Declaration and then repeated in the Convention on the Prevention and Punishment of Genocide adopted a day before the Universal Declaration.

On the concept of a 'human being', the eminent philosopher, Prof. Simon Blackburn has written that from Plato to Aristotle, "our capacities for reason have been seen as the crowning glory of humanity: the bit that sets us apart from other, 'lower' animals, and is even a special mark of divine favour."[14] It was expressly recognized during the drafting of the declaration that the words "all human beings" had been used precisely in order that both men and women might be included.[15]

When Rene Cassin's refinement of the initial draft by Humphrey was considered by the Drafting Committee, he told it that he had taken two leading ideas

11 Glendon op. cit., p. 58.

12 A/C.3/SR 98.,reproduced in Schabas, op. cit. p. 2173.

13 See on this S. Mumford, Metaphysics. A Very Short Introduction. Oxford, University Press, 2012, Chapter 7: What is a Person, esp. pp. 65-66.

14 S. Blackburn, What Do We Really Know. The Big Questions of Philosophy. London, Quercus, 2009, p.53.

15 A/C.3/SR. 98, reproduced in Schabas, op.cit., p. 2169.

as 'fundamental': ' that every human being has a right to be treated like every other human being' and 'the concept of solidarity and fraternity among men.' Cassin reiterated the point upon which he had insisted since the Commission's very first meeting: the declaration should base universal rights on the 'great fundamental principle of the unity of all the races of mankind'. Cassin later wrote that the main difficulty in framing the introductory 'General Principles', was "to find a formula that did not require the Commission to take sides on the nature of man and society, or to become immured in metaphysical controversies, notably the conflict among spiritual, rationalist, and materialist doctrines of the origin of human rights.".[16]

The affirmation of human rights for human beings would come to inspire efforts for the protection of minorities, indigenous peoples, children, women and persons with disabilities, among others. The project of the Universal Declaration was one of mutual respect and solidarity for every human being on the planet. This perspective would come to extend recognition of the humanity of tribes and indigenous peoples of all stripes.

On the concept of being free, it may be recalled that at the time when the United Nations Charter and the Universal Declaration were being drafted there had been popular movements for freedom and independence in places such as India, Indonesia, South Africa, Vietnam and elsewhere. The concept of freedom was undoubtedly linked with the Charter's concept of self-determination, which would give rise to the momentous decolonization movement and which would lead to a transformation of the world through recognition of the rights of all colonial and dependent peoples to freedom and self-determination.

The drafters of Articles 1 and 2 sought to register that human beings, by their very nature, should be free to develop to the fullness of their potential, with freedom to think, being in charge of themselves, without being subjected to slavery or subjection, without being in bondage to another, having personal rights and social and political liberty. The concept of freedom was universal, applying to all countries and peoples across the globe, to minority as well as majority populations, to women as well as men, to children, to minorities and indigenous peoples.

On the concept of equality, the factual claim is that human beings are equal; and the normative claim is that human beings should treated equally. The factual and normative claim, combined, lead to the claim that human beings ought to be treated as the equal beings that they in fact are. Bernard Williams has noted of the idea of equality, "It is their common humanity that constitutes

16 Glendon, op.cit., pp. 67-68.

their equality". While the idea of equality has been challenged by some prominent philosophers such as Robert Nozick, the international community, in the UN Charter, the Universal Declaration, and subsequent normative instruments, has, as a matter of international public policy, elevated the principle of equality into a norm of *jus cogens* in international law.

Kantian ethics had laid stress on the equal right of all human beings to treatment as ends in themselves as a foundation of all morality. During the drafting of the Universal Declaration, Hernan Santa Cruz (Chile) considered that Article 2 aimed above all at giving expression to one of the basic provisions of the Charter. The United Nations had been founded principally to combat discrimination in the world. It was essential to set forth in a separate article the basic postulates of the declaration, namely the principles of liberty, equality and fraternity .[17] Mr Ramirez-Moreno (Columbia), recognized that the philosophical basis of the phrase 'all human beings are free and equal' was fragile. ... It could be alleged that no equality existed, as men were not equally gifted or talented. Human equality, however, should be considered at a deeper level.[18] In other words, this was a matter of international public policy for the future.

The concept of dignity signifies worth, estimation. In modern moral philosophy, especially that of Kant, dignity is considered as a universal attribute, an offshoot of the capacity for self-consciousness and practical reason. The entrenchment of human dignity as a universal human rights norm was one of the great normative innovations of the 1940s. The UN Charter makes several references to the principles of the dignity and equality of all human beings. In the Preamble of the Charter, the Peoples of the United Nations reaffirmed their faith in fundamental rights, in the dignity and worth of the human person and in the equal rights of men and women.

During the drafting of the Universal Declaration, dignity as a right had been challenged by the representative of South Africa. Mrs. Roosevelt replied that the word dignity had been considered carefully by the Human Rights Commission, which had included it in order to emphasize that every human being is worthy of respect.[19] The Commission had decided to include it in order to emphasize the inherent dignity of all mankind.[20]

Turning to the concept of a right, Kant thought that the fundamental moral right is to be treated as an end in oneself, and reason alone justifies and grounds

---

17 A/C.3/SR 100, reproduced in Schabas, op. cit. p. 2196.
18 A/C.3/SR 98, reproduced in Schabas, op. cit.,p. 2171.
19 Glendon, op. cit., p.146.
20 A/C.3/SR 98, reproduced in Schabas, op. cit., p. 2169.

this right.[21] The Charter and the Universal Declaration began a process whereunder human rights norms are discussed, distilled, and proclaimed in consensual processes in authoritative international organs such as the UN General Assembly. The International Bill of Human Rights and the broader collection of United Nations human rights instruments are the outcomes of this process. This, in the stirring words of the late Louis Henkin, is an Age of Rights.[22]

The concept of reason signifies the Intellectual faculty characteristic of human beings by which conclusions are drawn from premises. Among philosophers the concept of reason has attracted a variety of positions. Brand Blanshard's definition of reason, in *Reason and Analysis,*[23] as "the faculty and function of grasping necessary connections" has been considered too narrow.[24] Some consider reason as being the faculty by the exercise of which we can perceive, or arrive, at truths of some particular kind. Reason may signify the careful weighing of arguments and evidence.

The concept of conscience signifies a moral sense of right or wrong as regards things for which one is responsible; a faculty or principle pronouncing upon moral quality of one's own actions or motives; reason or fairness: "The consciousness humans have that an action is morally required or forbidden"[25] As Mr Chang put it at one point during the drafting of the Universal Declaration, "The first condition for defence of the rights of man was tolerance towards the various opinions and beliefs held throughout the world. Uncompromising dogmatism had caused much harm, by accentuating disputes, and lending them an ideological basis ... If harmony was to be maintained in the human community and humanity itself was to be saved, everyone had o accept, in a spirit of sincere tolerance, the different views and beliefs of his fellow men.

"By pleading for tolerance of all opinions and beliefs and by insisting on precision of terminology, the Chinese delegation had striven to introduce certain improvements into the universal declaration of human rights."[26]

The concept of brotherhood signifies fraternal tie. During the drafting of the Universal Declaration, Mr Kayali (Syria), commented that the word brotherhood was an expression of the ideal moral relationship which should exist between men and meant that all men should behave to others as they would

21 Oxford Dictionary of Philosophy, op. cit.
22 L. Henkin, The Age of Rights op. cit.
23 Brand Blanshard, Reason and Analysis. London, 1962.
24 G.J. Warnock,"Reason", in The Encyclopedia of Philosophy. Paul Edwards, Editor in Chief, London, Macmillan, 1967, Vol. 7, pp. 83-85.
25 Oxford Dictionary of Philosophy, op. cit.
26 A/PV. 182, reproduced in Schabas, op. cit. p. 3058.

wish others to behave to them.[27] Mr Anze Matienzo (Bolivia), thought that there was no intention of claiming that human beings were perfect. The draft declaration was designed to set a goal for mankind. It should inspire men to transform into realities the principles it proclaimed.[28]

Mr Chang (China) commented that the second sentence of Article 1 called upon men to act towards one another in a spirit of brotherhood. That attitude was perfectly consistent with the Chinese attitude towards manners and the importance of kindly and considerate treatment of others. It was only when man's social behaviour rose to that level that he was truly human. Decorum was an ideal which should not be lost sight of – as unfortunately it was – in the struggle to uphold noble principles.[29] Mr Pavlov (USSR) (USSR) thought that a real spirit of brotherhood was possible only in the absence of exploitation of men by their fellow men, of weak nations by strong nations.[30]

The idea that every human being should be treated equally under the law and should be given equal access to opportunities is an article of faith of the UN and a bedrock principle of international human rights law. The inherent dignity and the "equal and inalienable rights of all members of the human family" were recognized in the UDHR's opening lines as the "foundation of freedom, justice and peace in the world."

Articles 2(1), 3, and 26 of the International Covenant on Civil and Political Rights set forth five related principles: the principle of equal enjoyment of rights; the general principle of equality and the corollary principle of equality between men and women; the principle of equality before the law and equality before the courts; the principle of equal protection before the law; and the principle of nondiscrimination. The covenant's preparatory works indicate that, notwithstanding differences in terminology, the principles of equality and non-discrimination in the document were intended to be the same principles as those contained in the Charter, the UDHR, and the International Covenant on Economic, Social, and Cultural Rights. The meaning of equality and non-discrimination in all of these instruments can be taken from the modern international law of human rights.

In the sections following we take up issues of equality, so closely related to the concept of justice.

---

27 A/C.3/SR 99, reproduced in Schabas, op. cit., p. 2184.
28 A/C.3/SR 98, reproduced in Schabas, op. cit., p. 2173.
29 A/C.3/SR 96, reproduced in Schabas, op. cit., p. 2152.
30 A/C.3/SR 98, reproduced in Schabas, op. cit., p. 2170.

5.1 *Equal Enjoyment of Enumerated Rights*

Article 2 of the ICCPR requires states parties to respect and ensure "the rights recognized in the present Covenant, without distinction of any kind, such as race, color, sex …" Unlike article 26, the article does not forbid distinction or discrimination generally, but only distinctions and discriminations in the enjoyment of the rights recognized in the covenant. But since the covenant recognizes equal protection of law (article 26), distinctions forbidden by the latter article also violate article 2(1).

Article 2(1) requires that the enjoyment of rights be respected "without distinction of any kind, such as race, color or sex." The clear implication is that the grounds enumerated are not exclusive, and other grounds for distinction are also barred. But the grounds barred are others similar to race, color "or other status." Even some types of "status" may be a permissible ground to deny rights if it is relevant. This includes, for example, being under age, mentally incompetent, and for some specified purposes, alienage. The covenant does not forbid depriving or limiting rights for misconduct, for example on conviction for crime.

5.2 *Non-Discrimination*

In addition to equality and equal protection, the covenant prohibits discrimination on particular grounds. Article 2 prohibits discrimination on forbidden grounds in respecting or ensuring the rights recognized by the covenant. Article 26 forbids discrimination on the same grounds in respect of equality before the law and the equal protection of the law. Discrimination on forbidden grounds is expressly prohibited also in the enjoyment of particular rights, such as the rights of children (article 18). Article 2 forbids discrimination in the enjoyment of the rights of the covenant. But article 26 forbids discrimination with respect to the equal protection of laws generally.

5.3 *Discrimination Versus Distinction*

During drafting, the question arose whether the word "discrimination" or "distinction" should be used. Ultimately, both words were used interchangeably, even within the same covenant. During consideration of article 26 of the Covenant on Civil and Political Rights in the Third Committee in 1961, some representatives stressed the differences between "discrimination" and "distinction."3 The following year, when article 2 (1) of the International Covenant on Economic, Social and Cultural Rights was being drafted, the Italian, Argentine, and Mexican delegations proposed an amendment to replace the word "distinction" with "discrimination" on the grounds that "some distinction might be Justified – for example, preferential treatment for certain under- privileged groups – and that it was discrimination which should be condemned."[4] Some delegations, however, argued that the proposal was questionable on legal grounds.[5]

In the end, however, it was decided to insert the word "discrimination" in the International Covenant on Economic, Social and Cultural Rights. When the Third Committee considered a similar provision of the International Covenant on Civil and Political Rights the following year, this same decision was not repeated. As a result, the International Covenant on Economic, Social and Cultural Rights uses the term "discrimination," and the International Covenant on Civil and Political Rights uses the term "distinction." It is clear from both debates that the drafters intended to include the higher level of protection, whichever word was used, in both covenants. Representatives proposing each word argued that it would give the higher level of protection. It is clear in the preparatory works of both covenants, however, that both terms exclude only arbitrary or unjust distinction or discrimination.[6]

A memorandum submitted by the division of human rights of the UN Secretariat to the Sub-Commission on Prevention of Discrimination and Protection of Minorities stated: "Discrimination implies, essentially, unequal and unfavorable treatment, either by the bestowal of favors or the imposition of burdens. Any of a number of grounds may underlie such unequal treatment." Four of them are mentioned in the Charter – race, sex, language, and religion. The prevention of discrimination is, therefore, the implementation of the principle of equality of treatment.[7] A later memorandum elaborated further: "The following delimitation of the meaning of the term discrimination may be suggested: discrimination includes any conduct based on a distinction made on grounds of natural or social categories, which have no relation either to individual capacities or merits, or to the concrete behavior of the individual person."[8]

The European Court of Human Rights, referring to the criteria for determining whether a given difference in treatment contravenes article 14 of the European Convention, has stated that:

> [T]he principle of equality of treatment is violated if the distinction has no objective and reasonable justification. The existence of such a justification must be assessed in relation to the aim and effects of the measure under consideration, regard being had to the principles which normally prevail in democratic societies. A difference of treatment in the exercise of a right laid down in the Convention must not only pursue a legitimate aim: Article 14 is likewise violated when it is clearly established that there

is no reasonable relationship of proportionality between the means employed and the aim sought to be realized.

5.4 *Affirmative Action*

When both covenants were being drafted, it was accepted that prohibiting discrimination or distinction does not preclude positive measures taken in favor of disadvantaged groups. When article 26 of the Covenant on Civil and Political Rights was being written, it was recognized that "the word, 'discrimination' ... was used ... in a negative sense only, to mean a distinction of an unfavorable kind." Similarly, it was said that the word "discrimination" conveyed the idea of a distinction made without any objective basis." The representatives of Chile, the Netherlands, and Uruguay pointed out that equality did not mean identity of treatment.

During discussions on the International Covenant on Economic, Social and Cultural Rights in 1962, the Indian representative pointed out that implementing non-discrimination raised certain problems, such as in the case of certain groups in under-developed countries. Thus, it was suggested that the committee add an article reading: "Special measures for the advancement of any socially and educationally backward sections of society shall not be construed as distinctions under this article." The committee endorsed the point made by the Indian representative, and the position adopted by the Third Committee followed that also made by the World Court in a case regarding minority schools in Albania.

5.5 *General Comment 4/13 of the Human Rights Committee (Gender Equality)*

In General Comment 4/13, of 28 July 1991, the Human Rights Committee provided important guidance on the international law of human rights regarding gender equality, specifically under articles 2 (1), 3, and 26 of the International Covenant on Civil and Political Rights. Importantly, the committee began with the observation that these articles require measures of protection but also affirmative action to ensure the positive enjoyment of rights. This cannot be done simply by enacting laws. Hence, more information has generally been required to ascertain what measures, in addition to law, are required to give effect to the obligations under article 3 and to ascertain what progress is being made or what factors or difficulties are being met in this regard. However, the positive obligation undertaken by states parties may have an inevitable impact on legislation or administrative measures designed to regulate matters other than those addressed in the covenant but which may adversely affect rights recognized in the covenant. As an example, the committee mentioned the degree to which immigration laws that distinguish between men and women may adversely affect women's rights to marry non-citizens or hold public office.

The Human Rights Committee advised that that it might assist states parties if special attention were given to a review by specially appointed bodies or institutions of laws or measures that inherently draw a distinction between men and women if those laws or measures adversely affect covenant rights. The committee also considered that it might help the states parties implement this obligation if more use could be made of existing means of international cooperation to exchange experience and organize assistance to solve the practical problems connected with ensuring equal rights for men and women.

5.6 *The Beijing World Conference on Women's Rights (1995)*

The fourth World Conference on Women's Rights, held in Beijing in September 1995, was a landmark in efforts to advance gender justice. The conference recognized that the status of women had advanced in some important respects in the previous decade. Nonetheless, progress had been uneven, inequalities between women and men persisted, and obstacles remained. The conference also recognized that the increasing poverty affecting many people, particularly women and children, exacerbated the situation.

The conference reaffirmed the commitment to equal rights and the human dignity of women and men enshrined in the UN Charter, the UDHR, and other international human rights instruments, in particular the Convention on the Elimination of All Forms of Discrimination against Women and the Convention on the Rights of the Child, as well as the Declaration on the Elimination of Violence against Women and the Declaration on the Right to Development.

5.7 *Equitable Life Chances*

The link between development and human rights has been prominent since the UN was established. Article 55 of the Charter set out the interdependence and interrelatedness of peace, development, and human rights. With a view to the creation of conditions which are necessary for peaceful and friendly relations among nations based on respect for the principle of equal rights and self-determination of peoples, the United Nations shall promote:

(a) Higher standards of living, full employment, and conditions of economic and social progress and development,

(b) Solutions of international economic, social, health, and related problems, and international cultural and educational cooperation;

(c) Universal respect for, and observance of, human rights and fundamental freedoms for all without distinction as to race, sex, language, or religion.

The importance of development for human rights and the need to integrate human rights in the development process have been emphasized since the Charter was drafted, and, currently, there are extensive debates about rights-based approaches to development and the role of human rights in poverty reduction strategies. While related, these are distinct from the right to development, and further examination of the substance of this idea, as well the different interpretations given by developing and developed countries, is required.

The World Conference on Human Rights reaffirmed the right to development, as established in the Declaration on the Right to Development as a universal and inalienable right and an integral part of fundamental human rights. (Vienna Declaration, paragraph 10)

The International Covenant on Economic, Social and Cultural Rights envisaged development performing six roles. First, development comes closest to being recognized as a right in article 11, which refers to the right to an adequate standard of living "and to the continuous improvement of living conditions." The covenant follows a deliberate scheme in which many articles define the right recognized and then proceed to indicate the steps to be taken, nationally and internationally, to promote rights such as the right to an adequate standard of living.

Second, development is sometimes cast, in some instances, as derivative of a recognized right. This is the case, for example, in article 1, which addresses the right to self-determination and also states that by "virtue of that right," people fully pursue their economic, social, and cultural development.

Third, development is cast as a goal to be pursued when trying to realize the rights recognized in the covenant. One may see this, for example, in article 15 on the right to take part in cultural life. This article specifies that states parties should include the "development and the diffusion of science and culture." Another example is article 13(2e), which includes "the development of a system of schools at all levels" among the steps to be taken to implement the right to education.

Fourth, in some instances, development is cast as a guide to implement a right recognized in the covenant. For example, article 12 on the right to enjoy the highest attainable standard of physical and mental conditions requires states to take steps "for the healthy development of the child." Likewise, article 13, after recognizing the right to education, adds that "education shall be directed to the full development of the human personality." (One might have thought that the "full development of the human personality" should have featured explicitly in the core definition of the right to development in the declaration adopted by the GA in 1986.)

Fifth, development is also included in the covenant as a means to realize the rights that the document recognizes. This is evident, for example, in article 6, which recognizes the right to work and specifies that the steps necessary to achieve this right should include "policies and techniques to achieve steady economic, social and cultural development." One also sees this in article 11(2a), which refers to the need for developing or reforming agrarian systems to achieve the most efficient development and utilization of natural resources.

Sixth, and finally, one sees the concept of development in determining the extent of a state's obligations to guarantee the covenant's economic rights to non-nationals.

The Declaration on the Right to Development (1986) in its Article 1(1), states that "the right to development is an inalienable human right by virtue of which every human person and all peoples are entitled to participate in, contribute to, and enjoy economic, social, cultural and political development, in which all human rights and fundamental freedoms can be fully be realized." One could also possibly include article 8 in this definition, which provided that:

1 States should undertake, at the national level, all necessary measures for the realization of the right to development and shall ensure, inter alia, equality of opportunity for all in their access to basic resources, education, health services, food, housing, employment and the fair distribution of income. Effective measures should be undertaken to ensure that women have an active role in the development process. Appropriate economic and social reforms should be made with a view to eradicating all social injustices.

2 States should encourage popular participation in all spheres as an important factor in development and in the full realization of all human rights.

Article 2(1) specifies that the human person is the central subject of development and should be the active participant and beneficiary of the right to development. Paragraph 3 of the same article adds that states have the right and duty to formulate appropriate national development policies. The possible subjects and beneficiaries are, therefore, the individual, the state, and all peoples.

In the Millennium Declaration, which was adopted on 8 September 2000, heads of states and governments reaffirmed their commitment to the UN Charter, expressing their determination to establish a just and lasting peace. Signatories to the document stated that the central challenge is to ensure that globalization is a positive force for the world's peoples. They considered certain fundamental values to be essential to international relations, such as freedom, equality, solidarity, tolerance, respect for nature, and shared responsibility.

In the document, governments declared their intention to spare no effort to free people from the scourge of war. They also resolved to strengthen the rule of law in international and national affairs and make the United Nations more effective in maintaining peace and security. The declaration stated that member states would spare no effort "to free our fellow men, women and children from the abject and dehumanizing conditions of extreme poverty." They resolved, in particular, to halve the proportion of the global population who live on less than one dollar a day, suffer from hunger, and lack access to safe water, all by 2015. They also committed to ensure that all children would be able to complete a full course of primary schooling. Similar goals were set to reduce maternal mortality, tackle HIV/AIDS and malaria, and improve the lives of slum-dwellers.

The declaration included the intention to protect the vulnerable and protect and assist children and civilian populations that disproportionately suffer the consequences of natural disasters, genocide, armed conflicts, and other humanitarian emergencies. They promised to make the United Nations a more effective instrument to pursue development and fight against poverty, ignorance, disease, injustice, terror and crime, and degradation and destruction of "our common home."

The Millennium Development Goals (MDGs) which were derived from the declaration. During the 1990s, a number of global conferences had taken place, defining the main objectives of the development agenda, now collectively known as the MDGs, which are eight goals to be achieved by 2015. Goal 8 called for a global partnership for development with the following targets:

- addressing the special needs of the least developed countries, landlocked countries and small island developing states;
- developing further an open, rule-based, predictable, non-discriminatory trading and financial system;
- dealing comprehensively with developing countries' debt;
- in cooperation with developing countries, developing and implementing strategies for decent and productive work for youth;
- in cooperation with pharmaceutical companies, providing access to affordable essential drugs in developing countries;
- in cooperation with the private sector, making available the benefits of new technologies, especially information and communications to developing countries.

6 The Human Rights Council's Contributions to the Global Quest for Justice

In this chapter, so far, we have discussed the decline of democracy in the world, the decline of human rights justice, the idea of justice in the philosophical literature, the idea of justice in the International Bill of Rights, and issues of equality. In the course of this book we have registered that the Human Rights Council is a political organ that takes decisions determined by the political complexions of its Membership, many of whom are undemocratic, and who often take unprincipled approaches. While the Council sometimes acts for justice for the victims of gross violations of human rights, many times it does not. The scales of the Council are therefore not evenly balanced. We have already argued that, for these reasons, one cannot say that the Council is an organ *of* justice.

Notwithstanding the fact that the Human Rights Council is a political organ that acts selectively or applies different weights and measures when responding to situations of gross violations of human rights, the Council still contributes to the global quest for justice in some ways, including the preparation of new human rights norms; the promotion of national protection systems through cooperation with National Human Rights Commissions and through the UPR process; contributing to the prevention of gross violations of human rights; providing a forum for airing grievances about alleged gross violations of human rights; sponsoring human rights fact-finding through its special procedures and commissions of inquiry; contributing to the protection of human rights defenders; sometimes condemning gross violations of human rights; sometimes calling for situations to be referred for the attention of the General Assembly and the Security Council and the International Criminal Court; sometimes calling for redress or compensation for the victims of gross violations of human rights. We have discussed these some of these contributions to the cause of justice in the different chapters of this book.

The Human Rights Council also provides a useful forum for seeking and promotion global justice, as we shall see next.

7 The Human Rights Council as a Forum for Seeking and Promoting Global Justice

The Human Rights Council provides a useful forum for NGOs and well-meaning governments to advocate for causes that otherwise might not be ventilated in the international community and to push for policies and recommendations aiming for global justice, or for justice for sections of humanity in dire need. A perusal of the resolutions and decisions of the Human Rights Council since its establishment shows it advocating for, and adopting resolutions and policy recommendations on issues such as:

- Climate change
- The environment
- Development
- Peace
- Combatting slavery and slavery-like practices, including human trafficking
- The plight of women and children
- Global hunger
- Access to medicine
- Access to safe drinking water and sanitation
- Protection against racism and racial discrimination
- World-wide violations of human rights such as arbitrary and extra-judicial executions, arbitrary detention, torture, enforced or involuntary disappearances, violence against women, human trafficking, persecution on grounds of religion or belief and similar gross violations of human rights.
- The quest of Afro-descendants for historical justice
- Protection of minorities
- Protection of Indigenous populations
- Protection of LGBTQ persons
- Protection of persons with Albinism

and numerous similar topics. This is a unique pro-justice function of the Human Rights Council. Space limitation would not allow us to discuss all of these topics. However, we take some illustrative issues below.[31]

7.1 *Global Hunger*

The Human Rights Council has consistently championed the right of everyone to food. In its resolution 13/ 4, for instance, adopted without a vote on 24 March, 2010, the Council reaffirmed that hunger constituted an outrage and a violation of human dignity and therefore required the adoption of urgent measures at the national, regional and international levels for its elimination. The Council encouraged States to mainstream a human rights perspective in building and reviewing their national strategies for the realization of the right to food for all, and to take steps to promote the conditions for everyone to be

31 The final chapter, below, also presents resolutions of the Council on other topics where the Council may be seen pursuing the cause of justice for the needy, or for groups at risk.

free from hunger and, as soon as possible, to enjoy fully the right to food and, where appropriate, to consider establishing appropriate institutional mechanisms in order to:

(a) Identify, at the earliest stage possible, emerging threats to the right to adequate food, with a view to facing them;
(b) Strengthen the overall national human rights protection system with a view to contributing to the realization of the right to food;
(c) Improve coordination between the different relevant ministries and between national and subnational levels of government;
(d) Improve accountability, with a clear allocation of responsibilities, and the setting of precise time frames for the realization of the dimensions of the right to food that require progressive implementation;
(e) Ensure adequate participation, particularly of the most food-insecure segments of the populations;
(f) Pay specific attention to the need to improve the situation of the most vulnerable segments of society.[32]

7.2 *Widespread Lack of Access to Medicine*

In its resolution 12/24 adopted without a vote on 2 October, 2009, the Human Rights Council recognized that access to medicine is one of the fundamental elements in achieving progressively the full realization of the right of everyone to the enjoyment of the highest attainable standard of physical and mental health. The Council stressed the responsibility of States to ensure access to all, without discrimination, of medicines, in particular essential medicines, that are affordable, safe, effective and of good quality.

The Council called upon States, at the international level, to take steps, individually and/or through international cooperation, in accordance with applicable international law, including international agreements, to ensure that their actions as members of international organizations take into due account the right of everyone to the enjoyment of the highest attainable standard of physical and mental health, and that the application of international agreements is supportive of public health policies that promote broad access to safe, effective and affordable medicines.

The Council encouraged all States to apply measures and procedures for enforcing intellectual property rights in such a manner as to avoid creating barriers to the legitimate trade of medicines, and to provide for safeguards against the abuse of such measures and procedures.[33]

---

32 Resolution 13/4, paras. 1,10.

33 Paras. 1-3, 6.

7.3 *Widespread Lack of Access to Safe Drinking Water and Sanitation*

In 2008, the Human Rights Council created the mandate of independent expert on human rights obligations related to access to safe drinking water and sanitation. After considering the first report of the independent expert, the Council, in its resolution 12/8, adopted without a vote on 1 October, 2009, expressed its deep concern that approximately 884 million people lacked access to safe drinking water and that over 2.5 million people did not have access to basic sanitation. The Council urged the implementation of the relevant development goals and called upon all States:

(a) To create an enabling environment to address the issue of lack of sanitation at all levels, including, where appropriate, by budgeting legislation, the establishment of regulatory, monitoring and accountability frameworks and mechanisms, the assignment of clear institutional responsibilities and the appropriate inclusion of sanitation in national poverty reduction strategies and development plans;

(b) To collect, at the appropriate levels, current, accurate and detailed information about sanitation coverage in the country and the characteristics of unserved and underserved households and to make this information available to all stakeholders;

(c) To develop, where appropriate, national and/or local plans of action, in cooperation with other stakeholders, in order to address the lack of access to sanitation in a comprehensive way, giving due consideration to wastewater management, including treatment and reuse;

(d) To ensure and promote access to information for, and the full, free and meaningful participation of, local communities in the design, implementation and monitoring of the above-mentioned plans of action;

(e) To adopt a gender-sensitive approach to all relevant policymaking in the light of the special sanitation needs of women and girls;

(f) To organize or otherwise support, as appropriate, large-scale public awareness campaigns promoting behaviour change in sanitation and to provide information, in particular on hygiene promotion.[34]

7.4 *World-Wide Discrimination Against Women*

The Council has repeatedly reaffirmed the obligations of States to take all appropriate measures to eliminate discrimination against women by any person, organization or enterprise. In this regard, it has expressed concern at the

34 Para. 5.

fact that, despite the pledge made at the Beijing World Conference on Women and the review by the General Assembly at its twenty-third special session, many laws that discriminate against women and girls are still in force and continue to be applied, thereby preventing women and girls from enjoying the full realization of their human rights. The Council has called upon States to fulfil their international obligations and commitments to revoke any remaining laws that discriminate on the basis of sex and remove gender bias in the administration of justice, taking into account that those laws violate their human right to be protected against discrimination.

The Council has deprecated the fact that women's inequality before the law has resulted in the lack of equal opportunities for women in education, access to health, economic participation, access to decision-making processes, inheritance, ownership of land, financial services, including loans, and nationality and legal capacity, among others, as well as increased vulnerability to discrimination and violence, and that all countries face challenges in these areas.[35]

7.5 *Child, Early and Forced Marriage in Times of Crisis, Including the COVID-19 Pandemic*

In a resolution that it adopted without a vote on 8 October, 2021, the Council expressed concern that child, early and forced marriage is underrecognized and underreported, and often coincides with impunity and a lack of accountability and access to justice, in particular at the community level, and that gender-biased environments promote impunity and impede the implementation of legislative and normative frameworks that guarantee gender equality and prohibit discrimination against women and girls. The Council urged States to respect, protect and fulfil the human rights of all women and girls, including those subjected to child, early and forced marriage.

The Council specifically urged States to take comprehensive, multisectoral and rights-based measures to prevent and eliminate child, early and forced marriage, including in times of crisis, and to address structural and underlying causes and risk factors, which the Council itemized in some detail.[36] The Council, furthermore, urged States to remove any provisions that may enable, justify, or lead to child, early or forced marriage, including provisions that enable perpetrators of rape, sexual abuse, sexual exploitation, abduction,

35 Resolution 12/17, adopted without a vote on 2 October, 2009.

36 Resolution 48/6, Child, early and forced marriage in times of crisis, including the COVID-19 pandemic, para.3.

trafficking in persons or modern slavery to escape prosecution and punishment by marrying their victims, in particular by repealing or amending such laws.

7.6 *Pervasive Gross Violations of Human Rights*

The Human Rights Council deals on an on-going basis with world-wide gross violations of human rights such as arbitrary and extra-judicial executions, arbitrary detention, torture, enforced or involuntary disappearances, violence against women, human trafficking, persecution on grounds of religion or belief and similar gross violations of human rights. The Council has some fifty 'special procedures' mandate-holders who study, investigate and report to the Council on these issues. Based on their reports, the Council regularly adopts resolutions deprecating these violations and offering recommendations for their discontinuance.

As an example, the Council has expressed deep concern that violations of the right to freedom of opinion expression continue to occur, including increased attacks directed against, and killing of journalists and media workers, and has stressed the need to ensure greater protection for all media professionals and for journalistic sources. The Council has reaffirmed the rights contained in the International Covenant on Civil and Political Rights, in particular the right of everyone to hold opinions without interference, as well as the right to freedom of expression, including the freedom to seek, receive and impart information and ideas of all kinds, regardless of frontiers, either orally, in writing or in print, in the form of art or through any other media of their choice, and the intrinsically linked rights to freedom of thought, conscience and religion, peaceful assembly and association and the right to take part in the conduct of public affairs.[37]

The Council has expressed continuing concern that violations of the rights referred to above continue to occur, often with impunity, including extrajudicial killing, arbitrary detention, torture, intimidation, persecution and harassment, threats and acts of violence and of discrimination, including gender-based violence and discrimination, increased abuse of legal provisions on defamation and criminal libel as well as on surveillance, search and seizure, and censorship against persons who exercise, seek to promote or defend these rights, including journalists, writers and other media workers, Internet users and human rights defenders.[38]

---

37 Resolution 12/16 adopted without a vote on 2 October, 2009.

38 Ibid.

7.7 *Afro-Descendants*

Following on the work of its predecessor, the Commission on Human Rights, the Human Rights Council has consistently advocated against racism and racial discrimination and championed the cause of Afro-descendants. It has a dedicated Working Group on this issue and has adopted important decisions on this topic.

According to a note published by OHCHR, people of African descent comprise a heterogeneous group with diverse histories, experiences and identities. The circumstances in which they live and the problems they fact differ. What unites them, however, is that they have long been denied the full realization of their human rights and one could highlight a series of common issues of justice that need to be addressed:

- Structural and institutional racial discrimination, xenophobia and related intolerance;
- Low levels of participation and underrepresentation in political and institutional decision-making processes;
- Lack of adequate representation in the administration of justice;
- Barriers to and inequality in the enjoyment of key human rights such as access to quality education, health services and housing, which results in the inter-generational transmission of poverty;
- Inequality in access to labour markets;
- Disproportionate presence in prison populations;
- Racial profiling;
- Limited social recognition and valuing of people of African descent's ethnic and cultural diversity and contribution to society;
- Intolerance against religions of African origin.[39]

The UN General Assembly, in its resolution 68/237, proclaimed the International Decade for people of African descent with the theme, recognition, justice and development. The Human Rights Council has a Working Group of Experts on People of African Descent which is mandated to study the problems of racial discrimination faced by people of African descent living in the African Diaspora. The Group, composed of five independent experts, undertakes activities such as the following:

- Presents annual reports to the Human Rights Council and the General Assembly;
- Prepares thematic reports on the protection of the rights of people of African descent;

39 OHCHR, Peoples of African Descent, undated; accessed on 12 April, 2021.

- Processes cases of alleged human rights violations of people of African descent through its petition procedure;
- Carries out country visits to review the human rights situations of people of African descent.[40]

7.8 *LGTBQs*

The Council has adopted a series of resolutions calling for respect for the human rights of all persons regardless of sexual orientation

7.9 *Albinism*

The Council has vigorously defended the human rights of persons with albinism, who have come under attack in places such as East Africa.

8 Conclusion

Discussing justice, liberty, and equality, the philosopher Mortimer Adler argued for the sovereignty of justice:

> [W]e must note the sovereignty of justice. It regulates our thinking about liberty and equality. Without its guidance, certain errors are unavoidable and certain problems insoluble. [J]ustice is the supreme value, a greater good than either liberty or equality, and one that must be appealed to for the rectification of errors with regard to liberty and equality.

He continued:

> Only justice is an unlimited good. ... One can want too much liberty and too much equality – more than is good for us to have in relation to our fellow men, and more than we have any right to. Not so with justice. No society can be too just; no individual can act more justly than is good for him or his fellowmen.

The arc of history, former US President Barrack Obama once said, bends towards justice. The challenge before the Human Rights Council, and the human rights community, is to strive constantly to increase the element of justice in the activities of the Council. This is, admittedly, no easy task. But there is no choice but to try.

40 Ibid.

CHAPTER 10

Jurisprudence

1 Introduction

In his classic work, Human Rights. Between Idealism and Realism,[1] Professor Christian Tomuschat, who has extensive experience with international human rights theory, law and practice, has an insightful discussion of 'Soft Law', particularly "a multitude of non-binding recommendations in the form of resolutions" of the UN General Assembly and the Human Rights Council. He considers that these efforts, which seek to elevate the level of protection in situations where, according to practical experience, violations of human rights are likely to occur, "not only have their legitimacy but also their usefulness."[2] He explains:

> Despite their lack of bindingness proper, the many resolutions seeking to particularize specific human rights guarantees have a tremendous influence on the development of the law. Generally, and almost ineluctably, domestic and international practice will adopt such resolutions as parameters guiding their actions. Progressively, then, a process of hardening into law can take place which one may either interpret as authentic interpretation of the relevant written rules or as the emergence of new rules of customary law. In any event, lawyers acting in a dispute before an international body of adjudicators would fail in their duties if they did not refer, in support of their arguments, to the existing soft law propositions among which the general comments and recommendations of the monitoring bodies acquire an ever-growing weight.[3]

The Human Rights Council is indeed, at its core, a political body and it could seem a stretch to speak of a jurisprudence of the Council, especially keeping in mind the deficiencies in protection to which we have alluded earlier in this book. Notwithstanding this caveat, we think that it is possible to identify some strands of what may be considered a jurisprudence of the Council. These strands may be in the form of clarifications, codifications, or contributions to the progressive development of the law. The hardness or the softness of the law

1 Oxford, University Press, Third Edition, 2014.
2 Ibid, p. 45.
3 Ibid, pp. 45-46.

 | DOI:10.1163/9789004504950_012

would need to be assessed in each instance. We offer below some illustrations of what may be considered contributions of the Council to the clarification, codification, or progressive development of international human rights law.

In presenting the materials that follow we are guided by the following considerations: first, we present the evidence while being fully cognizant that legal assertions may be interspersed with political slants. We do not contend that the political assertions necessarily represent statements of law; but we think that political slants should not obscure what are often manifest legal assertions. Second, we have in mind five categories of legal assertions: statements that endeavour to provide a legal framework for the fast-evolving world order, for example, the pronouncements below on the promotion of a democratic and equitable international order;[4] statements that are reaffirmations of existing law; statements that elaborate on the legal obligations of governments to implement provisions of international human rights law; statements that are codificatory of the law; statements that are efforts at the progressive development of the law.

2 The Architecture of International Law: Principles of the UN Charter

The Human Rights Council, on the occasion of the seventy-fifth anniversary of the United Nations, reaffirmed its commitment to the Purposes and Principles of the Charter of the United Nations, "and its interlinked and mutually reinforcing pillars of peace and security, development and human rights, which are the indispensable foundation of a more peaceful, prosperous and just world, and reiterates its determination to foster strict for those purposes and principles".[5]

The Council has affirmed that all States should promote the establishment, maintenance and strengthening of international peace and security and an international system based on respect for the principles enshrined in the Charter and the promotion of all human rights and fundamental freedoms, including the right to development and the right of peoples to self-determination. It urged all States to respect and to put into practice the Principles and Purposes of the Charter in their relations with all other States, irrespective of

4 See resolution 8/5, Promotion of a democratic and equitable international order.

5 Resolution 44/23, Contribution of respect for all human rights and fundamental freedoms to achieving the purposes and upholding the principles of the Charter of the United Nations, adopted by 41-0 with 6 abstentions. s.

their political, economic or social systems, or of their size, geographical location or level of economic development;

It has reaffirmed the duty of all States, in accordance with the Principles of the Charter, to use peaceful means to settle any dispute to which they are parties and the continuance of which is likely to endanger the maintenance of international peace and security, and encourages States to settle their disputes as early as possible, as an important contribution to the promotion and protection of all human rights of everyone and all peoples.[6]

3 Normative Instruments: Treaties and Declarations

The Human Rights Council has taken forward the standard-setting role of its predecessor and has so far contributed a fair set of new standards, including the following instruments eventually adopted by the UN General Assembly: the International Convention for the Protection of all Persons from Enforced Disappearances (prepared during the time of the former Commission); the Declaration on the rights of indigenous peoples (prepared during the time of the former Commission); the Optional Protocol to the International Covenant on Economic, Social and Cultural Rights (started during the time of the former Commission but brought to conclusion with significant negotiations in the Council); the Convention on the rights of disabled persons; the Optional Protocol to the Convention on the Rights of the Child providing a petitions procedure; A Declaration on the Right to Peace; and a Declaration on the Rights of Peasants; and a Declaration on human rights and training.

In addition to the instruments mentioned above, the Council has also adopted policy or normative statements on a broad range of issues that could well, in time, contribute to the codification or progressive development of international human rights law. We present below a selection of such policy or normative statements below, taken from resolutions or decisions of the Council or from the reports of its Special Rapporteurs. Normative principles put forward by Special Rapporteurs oftentimes come to be endorsed or adopted by the Council itself.

---

6 Resolution 15/13, Human rights and international solidarity, adopted 32 to 14 with no abstentions.

4 Principles on Human Rights and the Environment

The future of humankind depends on controlling climate change and on preserving and nurturing the natural environment. The Human Rights Council has a Special Rapporteur on human rights and the environment who consulted widely and presented to the Council a set of sixteen Framework Principles on Human Rights and the Environment.[7] In the introduction to the principles the Special Rapporteur, John Knox, explained that human beings are part of nature and their human rights are intertwined with the environment in which they live. Environmental harm interferes with the enjoyment of human rights, and the exercise of human rights helps to protect the environment and to promote sustainable development.

The framework principles, he added, summarize the main human rights obligations relating to the enjoyment of a safe, clean, healthy and sustainable environment. They provide integrated and detailed guidance for practical implementation of these obligations, and a basis for their further development as understanding of the relationship of human rights and the environment continues to develop. The framework principles, he continued, were not exhaustive: many national and international norms were relevant to human rights and environmental protection and the framework principles should not be interpreted as limiting or undermining standards that might provide higher levels of protection under national or international law.

The framework principles presented by the Special Rapporteur are presented below. We reproduce them without the detailed commentaries that accompanied them. We understand that the proposals of a Special Rapporteur do not have the same status as the pronouncements of the Human Rights Council. Still, proposals such as these are often the start of a process of progressive development of the law. In view of the capital importance of protection of the environment and the reversal of climate change, the proposals below of the Special Rapporteur take on added significance.

Principle 1

States should ensure a safe, clean, healthy and sustainable environment in order to respect, protect and fulfil human rights.

Principle 2

States should respect, protect and fulfil human rights in order to ensure a safe, clean, healthy and sustainable environment.

7 A/HRC/37/59, 24 January, 2018, Annex.

Principle 3
States should prohibit discrimination and ensure equal and effective protection against discrimination in relation to the enjoyment of a safe, clean, healthy and sustainable environment.
Principle 4
States should provide a safe and enabling environment in which individuals, groups and organs of society that work on human rights or environmental issues can operate free from threats, harassment, intimidation and violence.
Principle 5
States should respect and protect the rights to freedom of expression, association and peaceful assembly in relation to environmental matters.
Principle 6
States should provide for education and public awareness on environmental matters.
Principle 7
States should provide public access to environmental information by collecting and disseminating information and by providing affordable, effective and timely access to information to any person upon request.
Principle 8
To avoid undertaking or authorizing actions with environmental impacts that interfere with the full enjoyment of human rights, States should require the prior assessment of the possible environmental impacts of proposed projects and policies, including their potential effects on the enjoyment of human rights.
Principle 9
States should provide for and facilitate public participation in decision-making related to the environment, and take the views of the public into account 8in the decision-making process.
Principle 10
States should provide for access to effective remedies for violations of human rights and domestic laws relating to the environment.
Principle 11
States should establish and maintain substantive environmental standards that are non-discriminatory, non-retrogressive and otherwise respect, protect and fulfil human rights.
Principle 12
States should ensure the effective enforcement of their environmental standards against public and private actors.
Principle 13
States should cooperate with each other to establish, maintain and enforce effective international legal frameworks in order to prevent, reduce and

remedy transboundary and global environmental harm that interferes with the full enjoyment of human rights.

Principle 14

States should take additional measures to protect the rights of those who are most vulnerable to, or at particular risk from, environmental harm, taking into account their needs, risks and capacities.

Principle 15

States should ensure that they comply with their obligations to indigenous peoples and members of traditional communities, including by:

(a) Recognizing and protecting their rights to the lands, territories and resources that they have traditionally owned, occupied or used;

(b) Consulting with them and obtaining their free, prior and informed consent before relocating them or taking or approving any other measures that may affect their lands, territories or resources;

(c) Respecting and protecting their traditional knowledge and practices in relation to the conservation and sustainable use of their lands, territories and resources;

(d) Ensuring that they fairly and equitably share the benefits from activities relating to their lands, territories or resources.

Principle 16

States should respect, protect and fulfil human rights in the actions they take to address environmental challenges and pursue sustainable development.

In a resolution that it adopted on 8 October, 2021 by a recorded vote of 43-0, with 4 abstentions, the Council:

1. Recognized the right to a clean, healthy and sustainable environment as a human rights that is important for the enjoyment of human rights;
2. Notes that the right to a clean, healthy and sustainable environment is related to other rights and existing international law;
3. Affirms that the promotion of the human right to a clean, healthy and sustainable environment requires the full implementation of the multilateral environmental agreements under the principles of environmental law.[8]

8 Resolution 48/13: the human right to a clean, healthy and sustainable environment.

5 Human Rights and Climate Change

The Council has expressed concern that climate change poses an immediate and far-reaching threat to people and communities around the world and has implications for the full enjoyment of human rights. In this regard, it has recalled that the Vienna Declaration and Programme of Action reaffirmed the right to development, recognized that human beings are at the centre of concerns for sustainable development, and further recognized that the world's poor are especially vulnerable to the effects of climate change, in particular those concentrated in high-risk areas. The Council has warned that low-lying and other small island countries, countries with low-lying coastal, arid and semi-arid areas or areas liable to floods, drought and desertification, and developing countries with fragile mountainous ecosystems are particularly vulnerable to the adverse effects of climate change.[9]

In a resolution that it adopted on 8 October, 2021, by a recorded vote of 42 to 1, with 4 abstentions, the Council expressed its resolve to contribute towards ongoing efforts at all levels to address the adverse impact of climate change on the enjoyment of human rights, in the light of scientific data and assessments, and in a well-integrated manner that advances progress towards the implementation of the 2030 Agenda for Sustainable Development, the Paris Agreement and the United Nations Framework Convention on Climate Change, as well as towards the promotion, protection, realization and enjoyment of human rights by everyone everywhere.

The Council appointed a special rapporteur on the promotion and protection of human right sin the context of climate change. The Council also requested its Advisory Committee to conduct a study and to prepare a report, in close cooperation with the Special Rapporteur, on the impact of new technologies for climate protection on the enjoyment of human rights.[10]

6 The Right to Peace

The Council has reaffirmed that the peoples of our planet have a sacred right to peace. It has also reaffirmed that the preservation of the right of peoples to peace and the promotion of its implementation constitute a fundamental

9 Resolution 7/23, adopted without a vote on 28 March, 2008.

10 Resolution 48/14, "Mandate of the Special Rapporteur on the promotion and protection of human rights in the context of climate change."

obligation of all States; Furthermore, the Council has stressed the importance of peace for the promotion and protection of all human rights for all.[11]

The Council has stressed that the deep fault line that divides human society between the rich and the poor and the ever-increasing gap between the developed and developing worlds posed a major threat to global prosperity, peace, human rights, security and stability. It stressed that peace and security, development and human rights are the pillars of the United Nations system and the foundations for collective security and well-being.

The Council has emphasized that ensuring the exercise of the right of peoples to peace and its promotion demand that the policies of States be directed towards the elimination of the threat of war, particularly nuclear war, the renunciation of the use or threat of use of force in international relations and the settlement of international disputes by peaceful means on the basis of the Charter of the United Nations.

The Council underlined the vital importance of education for peace as a tool to foster the realization of the right of peoples to peace, and encourages States, United Nations specialized agencies and intergovernmental and non-governmental organizations to contribute actively to this endeavour.

The Council has resolved to address, in accordance with its mandate established by the General Assembly in its resolution 60/251, systematic and gross violations of the human rights of civilians in armed conflicts.

The Council encapsulated its approach to the right to peace in a draft declaration it submitted to the General Assembly that the latter adopted on 19 December, 2016 as the Declaration on the Right to Peace. In this Declaration, the General Assembly stated:

> Article 1: Everyone has the right to enjoy peace such that all human rights are promoted and protected and development is fully realized.
>
> Article 2. States should respect, implement and promote equality and non-discrimination, justice and the rule of law, and guarantee freedom f rom fear and want as a means to build peace within and between societies.
>
> Article 3. States, the United Nations and specialized agencies should take appropriate sustainable measures to implement the Declaration on the Right to Peace …

11 Resolution 14/3, adopted on a recorded vote of 31 to 14, with 1 abstention.

Article 4. International and national institutions of education for peace shall be promoted in order to strengthen among all human beings the spirit of tolerance, dialogue, cooperation and solidarity. ...

Article 5. Nothing in the Declaration on the Right to Peace shall be construed as being contrary to the purposes and principles of the United Nations. ...

7 Promotion of a Democratic and Equitable International Order

The Council has reaffirmed that everyone is entitled to a social and international order in which the rights and freedoms set forth in the Universal Declaration of Human Rights can be fully realized.[12] It has also affirmed that everyone and every people have the right to a democratic and equitable international order. Unfortunately, the emphasis here is only on the international order, whereas it should have been on both the international and the national orders. The Council also affirmed that a democratic and equitable international order fosters the full realization of all human rights for all.

The Council further affirmed that a democratic and equitable international order requires, *inter alia*, the realization of the following:

(a) The right of all peoples to self-determination, by virtue of which they can freely determine their political status and freely determine their political status and freely pursue their economic, social and cultural development;

(b) The right of people and nations to permanent sovereignty over their natural wealth and resources;

(c) The right of every human person and all peoples to development, as a universal and inalienable right and an integral part of fundamental human rights;

(d) The right of all peoples to peace;

(e) The right to an international economic order based on equal participat9ion in the decision-making process, interdependence, mutual interest, international solidarity and cooperation among all States;

(f) International solidarity, as a right of peoples and individuals;

(g) The promotion and consolidation of transparent, democratic, just and accountable international institutions in all areas of cooperation, in

12 See article 28 of the Universal Declaration.

particular through the implementation of the prgincipIes of full and equal participation in their respective decision-making mechanisms;

(h) The right to equitable participation of all, without any discrimination, in domestic as well as global decision-making;

(i) The principle of equitable regional and gender-balanced representation in the composition of the staff of the United Nations system;

(j) The promotion of a free, just, effective and balanced international information and communication order, based on international cooperation for the establishment of a new equilibrium and greater reciprocity in the international flow of information, in particular correcting the inequalities in the flow of information to and from developing countries;

(k) The promotion of an inclusive global technology and knowledge society directed towards bridging the technology and knowledge divide, promoting a universal, equitable and non-discriminatory access to knowledge and technologies;

(l) Respect for cultural diversity and the cultural rights of everyone;

(m) The right of every person and all peoples to a healthy environment and to an enhanced international cooperation that respond effectively to the needs of assistance of national efforts of adaptation to climate change, particularly in developing countries, and that promote the fulfilment of international agreements in the field of mitigation;

(n) The promotion of equitable access to benefits from the international distribution of wealth through enhanced international cooperation, in particular in international economic, commercial and financial relations;

(o) The enjoyment by everyone of ownership of the common heritage of mankind in connection to a public right of access to culture;

(p) The shared responsibility of the nations of the world for managing worldwide economic and social issues as well as threats to international peace and security that should be exercised multilaterally;

In the same resolution, the Council stressed the importance of preserving the rich and diverse nature of the international community of nations and peoples as well as respect for the universality of human rights, national and regional particularities and various historical, cultural and religious backgrounds, in the enhancement of international cooperation in the field of human rights.[13]

---

13 Resolution 8/5, Promotion of a democratic and equitable international order. Adopted on 18 June, 2008 on a recorded vote of 33 to 13 with 1 abstention.

The principal sponsor of this resolution was Cuba, and one might be forgiven for recalling the maxim of equity in English law: "He who comes to equity must come with clean hands." Voting against the resolution were: Bosnia and Herzegovina, Canada, France, Germany, Italy, Japan, Netherlands, Republic of Korea, Romania, Slovenia, Switzerland, Ukraine, United Kingdom of Great Britain and Northern Ireland. Abstaining were Ghana and Mexico. Voting in favour were: Angola, Azerbaijan, Bangladesh, Bolivia, Brazil, Cameroon, China, Cuba, Djibouti, Egypt, Gabon, Guatemala, India, Indonesia, Jordan, Madagascar, Malaysia, Mali, Mauritius, Nicaragua, Nigeria, Pakistan, Peru, Philippines, Qatar, Russian Federation, Saudi Arabia, Senegal, South Africa, Sri Lanka, Uruguay, and Zambia.

This resolution clearly did not make law instantly, views being so clearly divided. But might it represent the cries for justice of the great majority of developing countries whose people are living in dire poverty and want? Can the international law of the future ignore texts such as these when considering the future architecture and content of international law, order and institutions? Can international lawyers ignore the majority voices within the United Nations?[14]

8 Human Rights: International Cooperation and International Solidarity

The Council has reaffirmed that it is one of the purposes of the United Nations and also the primary responsibility of Member States to promote, protect and encourage respect for human rights and fundamental freedoms through, *inter alia*, inter alia cooperation.[15] Of some importance, it has reaffirmed "that, in addition to their separate responsibilities to their individual societies, States have a collective responsibility to uphold the principles of human dignity, equality and equity at the global level.". The Council:

(i) Urged all actors on the international scene to build an international order based on inclusion, justice, equality and equity, human dignity, mutual understanding and promotion of and respect for cultural diversity and universal human rights, and to reject all doctrines of exclusion based on racism, racial discrimination, xenophobia and related intolerance.

---

14 See, further, Alfred de Zayas, Building a Just World Order. Atlanta, Clarity Press, 2021.

15 Resolution 13/23, adopted without a vote on 26 March, 2010.

(ii) Reaffirmed the importance of the enhancement of international cooperation for the promotion and protection of human rights and for the achievement of the objectives of the fight against racism, racial discrimination, xenophobia and related intolerance.
(iii) Considered that international cooperation in the field of human rights, in conformity with the purposes and principles set out in the charter and international law, should make an effective and practical contribution to the urgent task of preventing violations of human rights and fundamental freedoms.
(iv) Reaffirmed that the promotion, protection and full realization of all human rights and fundamental freedoms should be guided by the principles of universality, non-selectivity, objectivity and transparency, in a manner consistent with the purposes and principles set out in the Charter.
(v) Emphasized the role of international cooperation in support of national efforts and in raising the capacities of Member States in the field of human rights through, inter alia, the enhancement of their cooperation with human rights mechanisms, including through the provision of technical assistance, upon the request and in accordance with the priorities set by the States concerned.[16]

The Council has called upon the international community to promote international solidarity and cooperation as an important tool to help to overcome the negative effects of current economic, financial and climate crises, particularly in developing countries. It has reaffirmed that the promotion of international cooperation is a duty for States, that "it should be implemented without any conditionality and on the basis of mutual respect, in full compliance with the principles and purposes of the Charter of the United Nations, in particular respect for the sovereignty of States, and taking into account national priorities."[17]

9 Guiding Principles on Business and Human Rights

The "Guiding Principles on Business and Human Rights: Implementing the United Nations 'Protect, Respect and Remedy' Framework" were developed by the Special Representative of the Secretary-General on the issue of human

16 Idem.

17 Resolution 15/13, Human rights and international solidarity, adopted 32 to 14 with no abstentions.

rights and transnational corporations and other business enterprises. The Special Representative annexed the Guiding Principles to his final report to the Human Rights Council.[18] They included an introduction to the Guiding Principles and an overview of the process that led to their development. The Human Rights Council endorsed the Guiding Principles in its resolution 17/4 of 16 June, 2011.

The Guiding Principles were grounded in recognition of (a) States' existing obligations to respect, protect, and fulfil human rights and fundamental freedoms; (b) The role of business enterprises as specialized organs of society and performing specialized functions, required to comply with all applicable laws and to respect human rights; (c) The need for rights and obligations to be matched to appropriate and effective remedies when breached.

The Guiding Principles have done much to define the role and responsibilities of businesses in promoting and protection human rights.

Among the 'Foundational Principles' are that:

> Business enterprises should respect human rights. This means that they should avoid infringing on the human rights of others and should address adverse human rights impacts with which they are involved (Principle 11)
>
> The responsibility of business enterprises to respect human rights refers to internationally recognized human rights – understood, at a minimum, as those expressed in the International Bill of Human Rights and the principles concerning fundamental human rights set out in the International Labour Organization's Declaration on Fundamental Principles and Rights at Work. (Principle 12).

The responsibility to protect human rights requires that business enterprises:
(a) Avoid causing or contributing to adverse human rights impacts through their own activities and address such impacts when they occur;
(b) Seek to prevent or mitigate adverse human rights impacts that are directly linked to their operations, products or services by their business relationships, even if they have not contributed to those impacts. (Principle 13).

The responsibility of business enterprises to respect human rights applies to all enterprises regardless of their size, sector, operational context, ownership and structure. Nevertheless, the scale and complexity of the means through which

18 A/HRC/17/31.

enterprises meet that responsibility may vary according to these factors and the severity of the enterprise's adverse human rights impacts. (Principle 14).

In order to meet their responsibility to respect human rights, business enterprises should have in place bodies and processes appropriate to their size and circumstances, including:

(a) A policy commitment to meet their responsibility to respect human rights;

(b) A human rights due diligence process to identify, prevent, mitigate and account for how they address their impacts on human rights;

(c) Processes to enable the remediation of any adverse human rights impacts they cause or to which they contribute.[19]

In furtherance of the Guiding Principles, the Human Rights Council established in 2011 the UN Forum on business and human rights which, in the words of OHCHR, is the world's largest annual gathering on business and human rights with more than 2,000 participants from government, business, community groups and civil society, law firms, investor organizations, UN bodies, national human rights institutions, trade unions, academia and the media. Over three days, participants take part in 60 + panel discussions on topics related to the Guiding Principles on Business and Human Rights, as well as business-related human rights issues.

The Forum is guided and chaired by the Human Rights Council's Working Group on Business and Human Rights, as provided for in Human Rights Council resolutions 17/4 and 35/7. The Forum is open to all relevant stakeholder groups, including States, the wider United Nations system, intergovernmental and regional organizations, businesses, labour unions, national human rights institutions, non-governmental organizations, and affected stakeholders.[20]

10 National Infrastructure

In resolution No. 12, adopted without a vote at its ninth session,[21] the Human Rights Council encouraged States to accomplish progressively a set of human rights voluntary goals that included the following:

19 See, further, OHCHR, Guiding Principles on Business and Human Rights. Implementing the United Nations 'Protect, Respect, and Remedy' Framework. Geneva, United Nations, 2011.

20 See, https://www.ohchr.org?EN/Issues/Business/Forum/Pages/ForumonBusinessandHumanRights.aspx.

21 Resolution 9/12, adopted without a vote on 24 September, 2008.

Universal ratification of the core international human rights instruments.

Strengthening of the legal, institutional and policy framework at the national level in order to ensure the promotion and protection of all human rights,

Establishment of human rights national institutions.

Elaboration of national human rights programmes and plans of action.

Adoption and implementation of programmes of human rights education

Strengthening national capacity to fight hunger and poverty.

Calls upon States to enact and, where necessary, reinforce or amend domestic legislation, including measures to enhance the protection of victims, to investigate, prosecute, punish and redress the wrongs done to women and girls subjected to any form of violence, whether in the home, the workplace, the community or society, in custody or in situations of armed conflict, to ensure that such legislation conforms with relevant international human rights instruments and international humanitarian law, constitute discrimination against women, to remove gender bias in the administration of justice, and to take action to investigate and punish persons who perpetrate acts of violence against women and girls

11 Protection of Human Rights While Countering Terrorism

The Council has reaffirmed that States must ensure that any measures taken to combat terrorism complies with their obligations under international law, in particular international human rights, refugee and humanitarian law; It has deeply deplored the suffering caused by terrorism to the victims and their families, expressed its profound solidarity with them, and stressed the importance of providing them with proper assistance.

The Council has reaffirmed its unequivocal condemnation of all acts, methods and practices of terrorism in all its forms and manifestations, wherever and by whomsoever committed, regardless of their motivation, as criminal and unjustifiable, and renewing its commitment to strengthen international cooperation to prevent and combat terrorism, and in that regard, called upon States and other relevant actors, as appropriate, to continue to implement the United Nations Global Counter-Terrorism Strategy, which, inter alia, reaffirmed respect for human rights for all and the rule of law to be the fundamental basis of the fight against terrorism.

The Council has further reaffirmed the obligations of States, in accordance with article 4 of the International Covenant on Civil and Political Rights, to respect that certain rights are non-derogable in any circumstances, and recalled, in regard to all other Covenant rights, that any measures derogating from the provisions of the Covenant must be in accordance with that article in all cases, and underlined the exceptional and temporary nature of any such derogations.[22]

12 Rights to Freedom of Peaceful Assembly and of Association

The Council has called upon States to respect and fully protect the rights of all individuals to assemble peacefully and associate freely, including in the context of elections, and including persons espousing minority or dissenting views or beliefs, human rights defenders, trade unionists and others, including migrants, seeking to exercise or to promote these rights, and to take all necessary measures to ensure that any restrictions on the free exercise of the rights to freedom of peaceful assembly and of association are in accordance with their obligations under international human rights law.[23]

13 Protection from Arbitrary Detention

The Council has encouraged all States:

(i) To take all appropriate measures to ensure that their legislation, regulations and practices remain in conformity with relevant international standards and the applicable international legal instruments.

(ii) To respect and promote the right of anyone arrested or detained on a criminal charge to be brought promptly before a judge or other officer authorized by law to exercise juridical power, and to be entitled to trial within a reasonable time or release.

(iii) To respect and promote the right of anyone deprived of his or her liberty by arrest or detention to bring proceedings before court, in order that the court may decide without delay on the lawfulness of his or her detention and order his or her release if the detention is not lawful, in accordance with their international obligations.

---

22 Resolution 7/7, Protection of human rights and fundamental freedoms while countering terrorism, adopted without a vote on 27 March, 2008.

23 Resolution 15/21, The rights to freedom of peaceful assembly and of association, adopted without a vote on 30 September, 2010.

(iv) To ensure that the right referred to in the sub-paragraph immediately above is equally respected in cases of administrative detention, including administrative detentions in relation to public security legislation.

(v) To ensure that anyone who is arrested or detained on a criminal charge has adequate time and facilities for the preparation of his or her defence, including the opportunity to engage and communicate with counsel.

(vi) To ensure that the conditions of pre-trial detention do not undermine the fairness of the trial.[24]

14 Protection of Human Rights Defenders

The Council has urged Governments to prevent and refrain from all acts of intimidation or reprisal against those who:

(a) Seek to cooperate or have cooperated with the United Nations, its representatives and mechanisms in the field of human rights, or who have provided testimony or information to them;

(b) Avail or have availed themselves of procedures established under the auspices of the United Nations for the protection of human rights and fundamental freedoms, and all those who have provided legal or other assistance to them for this purpose;

(c) Submit or have submitted communications under procedures established by human rights instruments and all those who have provided legal or other assistance to them for this purpose;

(d) Are relatives of victims of human rights violations or of those who have provided legal or other assistance to victims.

The Council has called upon States to ensure adequate protection from intimidation or reprisals for individuals and members of groups who seek to cooperate or have cooperated with the United Nations, its representatives and mechanisms in the field of human rights, and reaffirmed the duty of all States to end impunity for such actions by bringing the perpetrators, including accomplices, to justice in accordance with international standards and by providing an effective remedy for their victims.[25]

24 Resolution 15/18, Arbitrary detention, adopted without a vote on 10 September, 2010.

25 Resolution 12/3, Cooperation with the United Nations, its representatives and mechanisms in the field of human rights. Adopted without a vote on 1 October, 2009.

15 Right to Truth

The Council has recognized the importance of respecting and ensuring the right to the truth so as to contribute to ending impunity and to promote and protect human rights. It has encouraged States to consider establishing specific judicial mechanisms and, where appropriate, truth and reconciliation commissions to complement the justice system, to investigate and address gross violations of human rights and serious violations of international humanitarian law.[26]

Furthermore, the Council has:

1 Recognized the importance of respecting and ensuring the right to the truth so as to contribute to ending impunity and to promote and protect human rights;
2 Welcomed the establishment in several States of specific judicial mechanisms and other non-judicial mechanisms, such as truth and reconciliation commissions, that complement the justice system, to investigate violations of human rights and of international humanitarian law, and appreciated 5the elaboration and publication of the reports and decisions of these bodies;
3 Encouraged the States concerned to disseminate, implement and monitor implementation of the recommendations of non-judicial mechanisms such as truth and reconciliation commissions, and to provide information regarding compliance with the decisions of judicial mechanisms;
4 Encouraged other States to consider establishing specific judicial mechanisms and, where appropriate, truth and reconciliation commissions to complement the justice system in order to investigate and address gross violations of human rights and serious violations of international humanitarian law;
5 Encouraged States to provide requesting States the necessary and appropriate assistance regarding the right to the truth by means of, among other actions, technical cooperation and exchange of information concerning administrative, legislative and judicial and non-judicial measures, as well as experiences and best practices that have as a purpose the protection, promotion and implementation of this right, including practices regarding the protection of witnesses and the preservation and management of archives;

26 Resolution 9/11.

6 Also encouraged States to design programmes and other measures to protect witnesses and individuals who cooperate with judicial bodies and mechanisms of a quasi-judicial or non-judicial nature, such as human rights commissions and truth commissions;[27]

...

16 Transitional Justice

The Council has welcomed the importance and urgency of national and international efforts to restore justice and the rule of law in conflict and post-conflict situations and, where relevant, in the context of transitional processes. It has underlined the need for the rights of both victims and accused persons to be respected, in accordance with international standards, with particular attention paid to those most affected by conflicts and the breakdown of the rule of law, among them women, children, migrants, refugees, persons with disabilities and persons belonging to minorities and indigenous peoples, and to ensure that specific measures are taken for their free participation and protection and for the sustainable return of refugees and internally displaced persons in safety and dignity.[28]

17 Protection of Civilians in Armed Conflict

The Council, acknowledging that human rights law and international humanitarian law are complementary and mutually reinforcing, expressed deep concern at the violation of human rights during armed conflicts, and of international humanitarian law, which undermined the protection of civilians in armed conflicts. It called upon all States to respect the human rights of civilians in armed conflicts and stressed the importance of combating impunity in order to prevent violations of international human rights law and international humanitarian law against civilians in armed conflicts, and urged States, in accordance with their international obligations, to bring perpetrators of such crimes to justice.[29]

27 Resolution 12/12, Right to Truth, adopted on 1 October 2009 without a vote.

28 Resolution 9/10, Human rights and transitional justice, adopted without a vote on 24 September, 2008.

29 Resolution 9/9, Protection of the human rights of civilians in armed conflict adopted ...

18 Right to Food

The Council has reaffirmed that hunger constitutes an outrage and a violation of human dignity and therefore requires the adoption of urgent measures at the national, regional and international levels for its elimination. It has also reaffirmed the right of everyone to have access to safe and nutritious food, consistent with the right to adequate food and the fundamental right of everyone to be free from hunger, so as to be able to fully develop and maintain his or her physical and mental capacities.

The Council considers it intolerable that more than six million children still die every year from hunger-related illness before their fifth birthday and that there are about 854 million undernourished people in the world and that, while the prevalence of hunger has diminished, the absolute number of undernourished people has been increasing in recent years when, according to the Food and Agriculture Organization of the United Nations, the planet could produce enough food to feed 12 billion people, twice the world's population at the time of the adoption of the Council's resolution.

The Council has expressed its concern that women and girls were disproportionately affected by hunger, food insecurity and poverty, in part as a result of gender inequality and discrimination, that in many countries, girls are twice as likely as boys to die from malnutrition and preventable childhood diseases, and that it is estimated that almost twice as many women as men suffer from malnutrition. The Council has encouraged all States to take action to address gender inequality and discrimination against women, in particular where it contributes to the malnutrition of women and girls.[30]

The Council has also expressed grave concern at the worsening food crisis which, in its assessment, seriously undermined the realization of the right to food for all. It called upon States, individually and through international cooperation and assistance, relevant multilateral institutions and other relevant stakeholders, to take all necessary measures to ensure the realization of the right to food as an essential human rights objective, and to consider reviewing any policy or measure which could have a negative impact on the realization of the right to food, particularly the right of everyone to be free from hunger, before instituting such a policy or measure. The Council stressed that States have a primary obligation to make their best efforts to meet the

30 Resolution 7/14, The right to food, adopted without a vote on 27 March, 2008.

vital food needs of their populations, especially of the vulnerable groups and households.[31]

19 Human Rights and Access to Safe Drinking Water and Sanitation

The Council has called upon States:

(a) To create an enabling environment to address the issue of lack of sanitation at all levels, including, where appropriate, by budgeting, legislation, the establishment of regulatory, monitoring and accountability frameworks and mechanisms, the assignment of clear institutional responsibilities and the appropriate inclusion of sanitation in national poverty reduction strategies and development plans;

(b) To collect, at the appropriate level, current, accurate and detailed information about sanitation coverage in the country and the characteristics of unserved and underserved households, and to make this information available to all stakeholders;

(c) To develop, where appropriate, national and/or local plans of action, in cooperation with other stakeholders, in order to address the lack of access to sanitation in a comprehensive way, giving due consideration to waste-water management, including treatment and reuse;

(d) To ensure and promote access to information for, and the full, free and meaningful participation of, local communities in the design, implementation and monitoring of the above-mentioned plans of action;

(e) To adopt a gender-sensitive approach to all relevant policymaking in the light of the special sanitation needs of women and girls;

(f) To organize or otherwise support, as appropriate, large-scale public awareness campaigns promoting behaviour change in sanitation and to provide information, in particular on hygiene promotion.[32]

The Council has also called upon States:

(a) To prioritize in an appropriate way funding for safe drinking water and sanitation, with a particular focus on extending access to the unserved or underserved, including measures to identify the most marginalized, excluded and disadvantaged persons in terms of access to safe drinking water and sanitation, to develop the capacity of decision-makers

31 Resolution S-7/1, The negative impact of the worsening of the world food crisis on the realization of the right to food for all, adopted without a vote on 22 May, 2008.

32 Resolution 12/9, Human rights and access to safe drinking water and sanitation, adopted without a vote on 1 October, 2009.

and practitioners for implementing strategies and concepts specifically focusing on the sustainable provision of safe drinking water and sanitation to the unserved poor, and to develop specific initiatives that are more likely to reach the most marginalized and disadvantaged and improve their situation;

(b) To consider increasing the percentage of international aid allocated to safe drinking water and sanitation, and to incorporate a human rights based approach;

(c) To monitor the affordability of safe drinking water and sanitation in order to determine whether specific measures are needed to ensure that household contributions are and remain affordable by means of, inter alia, effective regulation and oversight of all service providers;

(d) To promote transparency of budgets and other funding, as well as of programmes and projects of all actors in the water and sanitation sector, in order to ensure an adequate basis for planning with regard to the most vulnerable and marginalized sectors of society and in order to inform decision-making and policymaking processes in both public and private sectors;

(e) To consult with communities on adequate solutions to ensure sustainable access to safe drinking water and sanitation;

(f) To ensure the sustainability of access to water and sanitation by, inter alia, capacity-building of Government authorities at all levels with regard to their responsibilities in the service delivery chain, adequate budgeting of costs, including costs of maintenance and establishing an adequate and effective regulatory system.[33]

20 Access to Medicine

The Council has recognized that access to medicine is one of the fundamental elements in achieving progressively the full realization of the right of everyone to the enjoyment of the highest attainable standard of physical and mental health. It has stressed the responsibility of States to ensure access to all, without discrimination, of medicines, in particular essential medicines, that are affordable, safe, effective and of good quality.[34]

33 A/HRC/21/2, adopted without a vote.

34 Resolution 12/24, Access to medicine in the context of the right of everyone to the enjoyment of the highest standard of physical and mental health. Adopted without a vote on 2 October, 2009.

21 Guiding Principles on Extreme Poverty and Human Rights

The Council has adopted a set of guiding principles on extreme poverty and human rights prepared by its special rapporteur on extreme poverty. The Council has encouraged Governments, relevant United Nations bodies and others to consider the guiding principles in the formulation and implementation of their policies and measures concerning persons affected by extreme poverty.[35]

22 Rights of Peasants

In 2018, the Human Rights Council submitted to the General Assembly a United Nations Declaration on the Rights of Peasants and Other People Working in Rural Areas. The General Assembly adopted this declaration in its resolution 73/165 adopted on 17 December, 2018. The Declaration consists of twenty extensive articles. Article 3 provides that:

1 Peasants and other people working in rural areas have the right to the full enjoyment of all human rights and fundamental freedoms recognized in the Charter of the United Nations, the Universal Declaration of Human Rights and all other international human rights instruments, free from any kind of discrimination in the exercise of their rights based on any grounds such as origin, nationality, race, colour, descent, sex, language, culture, marital status, property, disability, age, political or other opinion, religion, birth or economic, social or other status.

2 Peasants and other people working in rural areas have the right to determine and develop priorities and strategies to exercise their right to development.

3 States shall take appropriate measures to eliminate conditions that cause or help to perpetuate discrimination, including multiple and intersecting forms of discrimination, against peasants and other people working in rural areas.

35 A/HRC/21/11, adopted without a vote.

23 The Human Rights of Older Persons

The Council has recognized the challenges related to the enjoyment of all human rights that older persons face in areas such as prevention and protection against violence and abuse, social protection, food and housing, employment, legal capacity, access to justice, health support, long-term and palliative care, and that those challenges require in-depth analysis and action to address protection gaps. It has called upon all States to ensure the full and equal enjoyment of all human rights and fundamental freedoms for older persons, including by taking measures to combat age discrimination, neglect, abuse and violence, and to address issues related to social integration and adequate health care, bearing in mind the crucial importance of family intergenerational interdependence, solidarity and reciprocity for social development.

The Council has encouraged all States to conduct their age-related policies through inclusive and participatory consultations with relevant stakeholders and social development partners in the interest of developing effective policies creating national policy ownership and consensus-building. It has called upon all States to enhance their existing mechanisms related to the protection and promotion of human rights for older persons, including by adopting, as appropriate, legal or other dedicated mechanisms. It has encouraged all States to raise awareness of the challenges facing the enjoyment of all human rights by older persons, and to ensure that older persons receive information about those rights.[36]

24 Basic Principles and Guidelines on Development-Based Evictions and Displacement

In 2007, the Human Rights Council took note of a set of Basic Principles and Guidelines on Development-Based Evictions and Displacement presented to it by its Special Rapporteur on housing rights.[37] The Basic Principles noted that forced evictions constituted a distinct phenomenon under international law, and were often linked to the absence of legally secure tenure, which constituted an essential element of the right to adequate housing. Forced evictions shared many consequences similar to those resulting from arbitrarily displacement, including population transfer, mass expulsions, mass exodus, ethnic

36 A/HRC/21/23, adopted without a vote on 28 September, 2012.
37 A/HRC/4/18, Annex I.

cleansing and other practices involving the coerced and involuntary displacement of people from their homes, lands, and communities.

Forced evictions constituted gross violations of a range of internationally recognized human rights, including the human rights to adequate housing, food, water, health, education, work, security of the person, security of the home, freedom from cruel, inhuman and degrading treatment and freedom of movement. Evictions must be carried out lawfully, only in exceptional circumstances, and in full accordance with relevant provisions of international human rights and humanitarian law.

Forced evictions intensified inequality, social conflict, segregation and 'ghettoization', and invariably affected the poorest, most socially and economically vulnerable and marginalized sectors of society, especially women, children, minorities and indigenous peoples.

Development-based evictions included evictions often planned or conducted under the pretext of serving the 'public good', such as those linked to development and infrastructure projects (including large dams, large-scale industrial or energy projects, or mining and other extractive industries; land-acquisition measures associated with urban renewal, slum upgrades, housing renovation, city beautification, or other land-use programmes (including for agricultural purposes); property, real estate and land disputes; unbridled land speculation; major international business or sporting events; and ostensibly, environmental purposes. Such activities also included those supported by international development assistance.

Displacement resulting from environmental destruction or degradation, evictions or evacuations resulting from public disturbances, natural or human-induced disasters, tension or unrest, internal international or mixed conflict (having domestic and international dimensions) and public emergencies, domestic violence, and certain cultural and traditional practices often took place without regard for existing human rights and humanitarian standards, including the right to adequate housing.

25 Trafficking in Persons

The Council has repeatedly expressed its concern at the high number of persons, especially women and children, who are victims of trafficking being trafficked within and between regions and States. The Council has called upon States:

(a) To effectively enforce relevant laws on trafficking in persons by, *inter alia,* intensifying capacity-building and training, including human rights education and training, for all relevant stakeholders, including the police, immigration authorities, border patrol officials, labour inspectors, judges, prosecutors, lawyers, and tax authorities, as well as health and child welfare professionals, within available means;

(b) To strengthen the enforcement of their labour laws and, in particular, to specifically train and increase awareness of labour inspectors and other competent authorities in addition to allocating adequate resources so that they have the capacity to identify victims of trafficking during labour inspections of establishments where trafficked persons are likely to be exploited, including in small or informal establishments;

(c) To take appropriate measures to promote and protect the human rights of trafficked persons in all categories of work;

(d) To develop and support programmes and initiatives that motivate businesses to contribute proactively to prevent and combat trafficking in persons, such as awareness-raising initiatives, grievance mechanisms, risk assessment, product certification, labelling, monitoring and verification;

(e) To encourage increased transparency and due diligence in the recruitment practices of companies and suppliers within their supply chains;

(f) To undertake initiatives, including awareness-raising campaigns, to inform on the dangers of trafficking in persons, including trafficking in supply chains;

(g) To promote partnerships and engage the business community and civil society, including non-governmental organizations, in developing and implementing sustainable initiatives to prevent and combat human trafficking in supply chains, taking into account the views and experiences of trafficked persons in designing, implementing, monitoring and evaluating such initiatives.[38]

26 Mercenarism

The Council has reaffirmed that the use of mercenaries and their recruitment, financing, protection and training are causes for grave concern to all States and violate the purposes and principles of the United Nations Charter. The Council has requested all States to exercise the utmost vigilance against any kind of recruitment, training, hiring or financing of mercenaries by private

38 Resolution 23/5, adopted without a vote on 13 June, 2013.

companies offering international military consultancy and security services, and to impose a specific ban on such companies intervening in armed conflicts or action to destabilize constitutional regimes. The Council has called upon all States that have not yet become parties to the International Convention against the Recruitment, Use, Financing and Training of Mercenaries to consider taking the necessary action to do so.[39]

27 Conclusion

Elsewhere in this book we have seen a number of features of the Council at work: formal reaffirmation of universality, but with strong under-currents travelling in the opposite direction; a fair measure of protection activities, but with selectivity and with different weights and measures in some situations; a tentative approach to prevention of gross violations of human rights; some urgent and good offices actions; significant fact-finding into allegations of gross violations of human rights; reaffirmation of the right to remedies for gross violations but with uneven application of the principle; and the Council manifesting itself not as an organ of justice but an organ for justice.

In this chapter we have seen the Council: reaffirming support for the principles of the UN Charter and for the norms of international human rights law and international humanitarian law; offering statements that are codificatory of international human rights law; offering statements that go in the direction of the progressive development of international human rights law; calling for laws and policies to protect humanity and its habitat as well as to provide dignity to the poor and the needy.

In short, even in the midst of intensely political activities, one sees, nevertheless, significant law-making and jurisprudential activities that are worthy of note and of systematization. This dimension of the Human Rights Council has, so far, not received attention in the literature. The community of international lawyers would do well to pay attention to these law-developing and jurisprudential activities of the Council which may well count among its key long-term contributions to the further development of international human rights law and jurisprudence.

39 Resolution 24/13, The use of mercenaries as a means of violating human rights and impeding the exercise of the right of peoples to self-determination, adopted by a recorded vote of 31 to 15 with 1 abstention.

Conclusion

The protection of human rights world-wide is vital for the realization of peace, development and justice. And yet, the promotion and protection of human rights at the United Nations are heavily politicized, with powerful and influential nations openly challenging the universality of human rights.

The UN Agenda 2030, and its related Sustainable Development Goals, envisage the world organization striving for national and international structures that can foster peace, development, justice, human rights and equitable institutions. This is the specific aim of SDG 16, which has a preventive rationale, grounded in justice and good governance. The implementation of this goal, to date, has moved at a snail's pace and has been even further slowed down by the COVID-19 pandemic.

The UN Human Rights Council was established with a mandate to promote and protect human rights world-wide and to act for the prevention of gross violations of those rights. It has its merits as well as its defaults. But, next to the Security Council and the General Assembly, it is the highest organ of the international community with a mandate to act for the universal promotion and protection of human rights. International lawyers must continue to place it under scrutiny and to assess its contributions to the international law of human rights.

The Human Rights Council is by its nature a political body. But, as Rosalyn Higgins demonstrated years ago in her book on the UN General Assembly and the development of international law, even political organs may play a role in the development of international law. One does see some evidence of this in the Human Rights Council.

In her inaugural address to the Human Rights Council on 8 February,2021, the incoming President of the Council, Ambassador Nazhat Shameem Khan, declared: "I commit to you all that I will bring to the Council a determination to maintain both impartiality and inclusivity. Above all, I will bring to the Council a commitment to further and to strengthen human rights everywhere. At this time, in this moment in history, strengthening the enjoyment of human rights, promoting and protecting the inherent dignity of all people, and placing equality and non-discrimination at the centre of sustainable development, are all of compelling importance." She added: "I commit to do my best in serving you all and I look forward to working with you in ensuring that this year remains a success, not just for the work of this Council, but also for the promotion and protection of human rights for all our people."

 | DOI:10.1163/9789004504950_013

Before proceeding to offer some assessments on the protection role and jurisprudence of the Human Rights Council, it would be useful to bear in mind some insights into the expectations of human rights NGOs at the outset of the 46th session of the Council. President Khan participated in a global internet meeting with human rights organizations on 9 February.[1] In her remarks, she pledged to strive for greater inclusivity and accountability in the Council. She considered civil society to be the voice and the conscience of the Council. On the occasion, an Indian human rights defender, Director of the NGO, Forum-Asia, addressing President Khan, highlighted the need to protect human rights defenders. She stressed the importance of civil society participation in the Council and made the telling point: "As Asia lacks a human rights forum, it needs the Human Rights Council."

An African human rights leader, speaking as the representative of human rights defenders' organizations, noted, in similar vein, that for many African countries domestic protection was sadly lacking and therefore human rights defenders looked to the Human Rights Council for protection. She considered that the Human Rights Council's Universal Periodic Review process could potentially empower civil society and could serve as a bridge between civil society and the international community. She thought that the leadership role of President Khan would be of great importance.

During the ensuing discussion with President Khan, representatives of human rights organizations made the following points to her:

- The importance of facilitating civil society participation in the Council
- The leadership role that the Council could play in dealing with the challenges of climate change
- The Council should recognize the human right to a healthy environment
- The Council's crucial role in acting for the protection of human rights in the COVID situation.
- The need to redress the digital divide between countries
- The crucial role of the Council in protecting human rights defenders.

Speakers at the meeting underlined the important role of the President in leading the process of protecting people victimised for speaking up for human rights in numerous countries in the world. A month later, at the concluding session of the 46th session of the Council, President Khan stressed, in her concluding remarks, that any act of intimidation or reprisal against those cooperating with the United Nations was unacceptable.[2] Whether Governments

1 The author was a participant in this Zoom meeting.

2 UN Press Release,"Human Rights Council Concludes Forty-Sixth Regular Session after Adopting 30 Resolutions and One Decision", 24 March, 2021, p. 2.

violating human rights paid any attention to this admonition was an open question.

Against this background of civil society expectations of the Human Rights Council, we may now turn to some conclusions that may be drawn from the previous chapters on the protection role and jurisprudence of the Council. Those conclusions may be summarised as follows:

1 *Universality*: The Council's founding resolution requires it to act on the basis of the universality of human rights and their interdependence. The universality of human rights is the formal basis on which the Council operates the Universal Periodic Review process, and all participating States, the entire membership of the United Nations, declare in their national reports that they subscribe to the universality of human rights. Nevertheless, there continue to be covert and overt challenges to universality by powerful States such as China, Russia, and even the Administration of former US President Donald Trump. China openly contests the accumulated rules and principles of international law, including on human rights. The Trump Administration in the USA had challenged the inherency and inalienability of rights declared in the Universal Declaration but its successor, the Biden Administration, has moved away from that challenge. The world organization has so far held the formal line on the universality of human rights. But this can be expected to be a central part of the power struggle between China and the United States as they vie for ascendancy in the global order of the future.
2 *Protection:* The protection of human rights may be anticipatory or preventive, mitigatory or curative, remedial or compensatory. Some protection work does take place under the auspices of the Council, notably by its Special Procedures or by the High Commissioner for Human Rights. But the Council itself is a politicized, selective body, that may or may not take up situations of alleged gross violations of human rights, depending on political lobbying among its Member States. We saw that a country, Cameroon, whose government has been grossly violating human rights for years, was nevertheless elected as a Member of the Council with the result that the Council failed to take up allegations of gross violations of human rights within the country at its 46th session. On a scale of one to ten, it would be hard to rate the Council above five as a protection actor.
3 *Prevention:* The preventive role of the Council is still largely undeveloped. Special sessions may or may not serve a preventive role. We

saw that the Council, just prior to its 46th session, held a special session on the situation of human rights in Myanmar with no tangible result whatsoever. To the contrary, the army of Myanmar, which had toppled a popularly elected government, proceeded to shoot down by the hundreds young people peacefully demonstrating in favour of democracy. Some actions of Special Procedures and of the High Commissioner for Human Rights may serve a preventive purpose from time to time. But, overall, one cannot say that the Council, as such, performs a preventive role except to the extent that its work for human rights overall might contribute to prevention in the long term.

4 *Urgent Action:* The special sessions of the Council are, indeed, a form of urgent action. But neither the President of the Council, nor its Bureau, has yet developed a preventive role. One does see some urgent actions by the Special Procedures and by the High Commissioner. One would be hard pressed to rate the preventive role of the Council at more than three out of ten.

5 *Good Offices:* The practice of humanitarian good offices within the framework of the Council is negligible except in three instances: actions by the President for the protection of human rights defenders, and intercessions by Special Procedures mandate-holders and the High Commissioner. One may rate this at two out of ten.

6 *Fact-Finding:* There is laudable fact-finding activity within the framework of the Council, undertaken by Special Procedures mandate-holders, the High Commissioner, and by designated fact-finding bodies such as the Commission on Human Rights in South Sudan. One would have to rate this fact-finding activity highly, possibly seven out of ten.

7 *Redress:* Limited redress takes place within the Council. The adoption of resolutions expressing concern over alleged gross violations, or condemning them, may be considered a form of redress, albeit a limited one. The Council has been willing to call for the referral of the occasional situation to the International Criminal Court. More recently, it has been developing the practice of asking the High Commissioner to gather and preserve evidence of gross violations for eventual justice processes, such as criminal trials or truth and justice commissions.

8 *Justice:* We have argued in this book that the Council is not an organ of justice, but an organ sometimes striving for global justice. The scales of justice must be evenly held. The Council is far from the keeper of a balanced scale of justice. However, it does strive for justice for the poor, the needy, and the disadvantaged. As a matter of principle, it

should strive to be both an organ of justice and an organ for justice. It is nowhere near the former.

9 *Jurisprudence:* There are four areas in which the Council has put down a significant jurisprudence: first a jurisprudence in respect of the national responsibility to protect human rights. Second, a jurisprudence in respect of thematic violations of human rights such as arbitrary and extra-judicial executions, torture, violence against women, enforced and involuntary disappearances, and arbitrary detention. Resolutions of the Council, building on the work of its predecessor, the Commission on Human Rights, have established benchmarks for national and international protection. Third, a jurisprudence in respect of global threats to humanity, such as climate change. Fourth, a jurisprudence calling for justice for the poor, the needy, and the disadvantaged.

What overall conclusion may we draw about the protection role and jurisprudence of the Council? At the end of the day, the world needs a body like the Human Rights Council. The Council has a noble mandate. Even if it often does it selectively, it does do some good. The challenge is to find ways of helping the Council to do better. The human rights community must keep pressing for more principled action by the Council to protect human rights world-wide. Based on the work done within the Universal Periodic Review process, one could target the adequacy and effectiveness of the national protection system of every Member State of the United Nations. With all the politicization inside the Council, it can still play a part in contributing to the strengthening of national protection systems inside every country. The High Commissioner for Human Rights, and the broader human rights community, can play a crucial role in helping the Council target the enhancement of national protection systems.

Bibliography

Abebe, Allehone Mulugeta, Human Rights in the Context of Disasters: The Special Session of the UN Human Rights Council on Haiti (February 23, 2011). Journal of Human Rights, Vol. 10, No. 1, pp. 99–111, 2011, Available at SSRN: https://ssrn.com/abstract=1768196.

Abebe, Allehone Mulugeta, Of Shaming and Bargaining: African States and the Universal Periodic Review of the United Nations Human Rights Council (February 13, 2009). Human Rights Law Review, Vol. 9, No. 1, February 2009, Available at SSRN: https://ssrn.com/abstract=1662808.

Alston, Philip and Morgan-Foster, Jason, The Competence of the UN Human Rights Council and its Special Procedures in Relation to Armed Conflicts: Extrajudicial Executions in the 'War on Terror' (February 1, 2008). European Journal of International Law, Vol. 19, No.1, pp. 183–209, 2008, Available at SSRN: https://ssrn.com/abstract=1149061 or http://dx.doi.org/10.1093/ejil/chn006.

Alston, Philip, "Reconceiving The UN Human Rights Regime: Challenges Confronting The New UN Human Rights Council," *Melbourne Journal of International Law*, vol. 7 (2006).

Anderson, Kenneth, Disengage and Obstruct: The UN-of-Values and the Human Rights Council (April 17, 2012). Living with the UN: American Responsibilities and International Order, pp. 207–256, Hoover Institution Press/Stanford University, 2012, American University, WCL Research Paper No. 2012-17, Available at SSRN: https://ssrn.com/abstract=2039746.

Boreham, Kevin, A Failure to Protect: The UN Human Rights Council and Darfur (April 26, 2010). ANU College of Law Research Paper No. 10-07, Available at SSRN: https://ssrn.com/abstract=1596392 or http://dx.doi.org/10.2139/ssrn.1596392 Chang, Jean. International Humanitarian Law in the Universal Periodic Review of the UN Human Rights Council: An Empirical Survey, " Journal of East Asia and International Law, Vol. 8, Issue 2 (Autumn 2015) , pp. 549–.

Chetail, Vincent, The Human Rights Council and the Challenges of the United Nations System on Human Rights: Towards a Cultural Revolution? (December 20, 2009). International Law and the Quest for Its Implementation: Liber Amicorum, pp. 193–241, V. Gowlland-Debbas, L. Boisson de Chazournes & M. Kohen, eds., Brill, 2010, Available at SSRN: https://ssrn.com/abstract=1647746.

Chetail, Vincent, The Human Rights Council: A Reform Without Change? (July 19, 2007). Conflits, Sécurité Et Coopération, pp. 125–167, Victor-Yves Ghebali, V. Chetail, ed., Bruylant, 2007, Available at SSRN: https://ssrn.com/abstract=1645139.

Chilton, Adam and Golan-Vilella, Robert, Did the Creation of the United Nations Human Rights Council Produce a Better 'Jury'? (October 18, 2016). U of Chicago,

Public Law Working Paper No. 597, University of Chicago Coase-Sandor Institute for Law & Economics Research Paper No. 780, Available at SSRN: https://ssrn.com/abstract=2860204 or http://dx.doi.org/10.2139/ssrn.2860204.

Devereux, A. (2021) 'Amidst Simmering Tensions: Improving the Effectiveness and Coherence of the International Human Rights System's Response to Mass Human Rights Violations', Australian Year Book of International Law, 38(1), pp. 199–229.

Dina, N. (2011) 'Human Rights Council Trampling on Rights: Finding Israel's Blockade Legal Underpins the Core Argument of the United Nations Report Condemning Israel's Attacks on the Flotilla', Southwestern Journal of International Law, 18(1), pp. 347–368.

Etone, Damien. The Human Rights Council: The Impact of the Universal Periodic Review in Africa. London, Routledge, 2020.

Freedman, Rosa, Failing to Protect. The UN and the Politicisation of Human Rights. London, Hurst and Co., 2014.

Freedman, Rosa, New Mechanisms of the UN Human Rights Council (February 2011). Netherlands Quarterly of Human Rights, Vol. 29/3 (2011), Available at SSRN: https://ssrn.com/abstract=2338595 .

Freedman, Rosa, The United Nations Human Rights Council: More of the Same? (March 24, 2015). 'The United Nations Human Rights Council: More of the same?', 31 (2) Wisconsin Journal of International Law (2013), 209–251, Available at SSRN: https://ssrn.com/abstract=2584385.

Freedman, Rosa, The United States and the U.N. Human Rights Council: An Early Assessment (August 2009). 23(1) St Thomas Law Review (2010), 23–70, Available at SSRN: https://ssrn.com/abstract=2338623.

Gerber, Paula, The Hitch Hiker's Guide to the New United Nations Human Rights Council (February 19, 2009). 10 Flinders Journal of Law Refrm 241, Monash University Faculty of Law Legal Studies Research Paper No. 2007/02, Available at SSRN: https://ssrn.com/abstract=1346722.

Hannum, Hurst, Rescuing Human Rights. A radically moderate approach. Cambridge, University Press, 2019.

Harrington, Joanna, Canada and the United Nations Human Rights Council: Dissent and Division (2009). [2009] 60 University of New Brunswick Law Journal 78–115, Available at SSRN: https://ssrn.com/abstract=3303805.

Harwood, Catherine, Human Rights in Fancy Dress? The Use of International Criminal Law by Human Rights Council Commissions of Inquiry in Pursuit of Accountability (July 6, 2015). (2015) 58 Japanese Yearbook of International Law 71–100, Grotius Centre Working Paper 2015/043-ICL, Available at SSRN: https://ssrn.com/abstract=2627058.

Henne, P. S. (2018) 'Does the UN Human Rights Council Help or Hurt Religious Repression?', Journal of Church & State, 60(4), pp. 705–724. doi: 10.1093/jcs/csy005.

Human Rights Council and Others v Ethiopia; African Commission on Human and Peoples' Rights Communication 445/13 (2015)' (2016) Mekelle University Law Journal, 4, pp. 153–176.

Jenks, Chris, Monitoring, Reporting, and Fact-Finding: Does the Human Rights Council Report on Human Rights in North Korea Provide a Template for the Sri Lankan Investigation? (April 28, 2014). PHAP Thematic Notes, 2014, SMU Dedman School of Law Legal Studies Research Paper No. 154, Available at SSRN: https://ssrn.com/abstract=2546381.

Jordaan, Eduart. South Africa and the UN Human Rights Council: The Fate of the Liberal Order. London, Routledge, 2019.

Joseph, Sarah and Jenkin, Eleanor, The United Nations Human Rights Council: Is the United States Right to Leave this Club? (April 9, 2019). 35 Am. U. Int'l. L. Rev. 79 (2019), Available at SSRN: https://ssrn.com/abstract=3368992 or http://dx.doi.org/10.2139/ssrn.3368992.

Karim, M. F. (no date) 'The limits of global human rights promotion: Indonesia's ambivalent roles in the UN Human Rights Council', Contemporary Politics, 26(3), pp. 351–370.

Kettemann, Matthias C., The UN Human Rights Council Resolution on Human Rights on the Internet: Boost or Bust for Online Human Rights Protection? (September 1, 2012). Human Security Perspectives 1/2012, 145–169, Available at SSRN: https://ssrn.com/abstract=2199431.

Lewis, Tamara, The Procedures of the United Nations Human Rights Council (December 19, 2015). International Human Rights Perspectives from Ireland, Suzanne Egan, editor, Bloomsbury 2015., Available at SSRN: https://ssrn.com/abstract=3055837.

Liljeblad, Jonathah, "Beyond Transnational Advocacy: Lessons from Engagement of Myanmar Indigenous Peoples with the UN Human Rights Council Universal Periodic Review, Vermont Law Review, Vol. 43, 2018, pp. 217–224.

Lloret-Blackburn, Roger, Cultural Relativism in the Universal Periodic Review of the Human Rights Council (September 1, 2011). International Catalan Institute for Peace, Working Paper No. 2011/3, Available at SSRN: https://ssrn.com/abstract=2033134 or http://dx.doi.org/10.2139/ssrn.2033134.

Lussenden, Ashleigh and Lee-Nakayama, Blaire and von Nagy, Helena and Fletcher, Laurel E., Human Rights without Support of the Concerned State: A Comparative Analysis of Successive Human Rights Council Mechanisms Established for Burundi and Myanmar (November 2020). IHRLC Working Paper Series No. 6, November 2020, Available at SSRN: https://ssrn.com/abstract=3742467 or http://dx.doi.org/10.2139/ssrn.3742467.

Mack, Raneta Lawson, China's Role on the New U.N. Human Rights Council: A Positive Shift in its Human Rights Agenda or a Marriage of Convenience? (April 21, 2007).

Maitya, J. (2010) 'Repositioning the International Human Rights Protection System: The UN Human Rights Council', Commonwealth Law Bulletin, 36(2), pp. 313–324.

Meng, S. and Haina, L. (2020) 'China and the Special Procedures of the UN Human Rights Council: Is China Cooperative and Can They Work Better With Each Other?', Human Rights Quarterly, 42(2), pp. 357–391. doi: 0.1353/hrq.2020.0021.

Merindol Ouoba, Clarisse. Le Conseil des droits de l'homme et ses principaux mécanismes: Bilan et perspectives d'actions pour le Burkina Faso à l'entame de son second mandat de membre, Paris, Editions l'Harmattan, 2013.

Mutua, Makau, Just Back from the Human Rights Council (2008). American Society of International Law, Proceedings of the 102nd Annual Meeting, pp. 329–33, 2008, Available at SSRN: https://ssrn.com/abstract=1533459.

Rajagopal, Balakrishnan, Lipstick on a Caterpillar? Assessing the New U.N. Human Rights Council Through Historical Reflection. Buffalo Human Rights Law Review, Vol. 13, No. 7, 2007, pp.7–16 Available at SSRN: https://ssrn.com/abstract=1032685.

Ramcharan, Bertrand, The Law, Policy and Politics of the UN Human Rights Council, Leiden, Martinus Nijhoff, 2015.

Ramcharan, Bertrand, The UN Human Rights Council. London, Routledge, 2011.

Renouard, J. (2020) 'Sino-Western relations, political values, and the Human Rights Council', Journal of Transatlantic Studies, 18(1), p. 80.

Richardson, L. (2015) 'Economic, Social and Cultural Rights (and beyond) in the UN Human Rights Council', Human Rights Law Review, 15(3), pp. 409–440.

Richemond-Barak, Daphné, The Human Rights Council and the Convergence of Humanitarian Law and Human Rights Law (March 4, 2012). Shaping A Global Legal Framework for Counterinsurgency: New Directions in Asymmetric Warfare, William Banks, ed., Oxford Univ. Press, 2012, Available at SSRN: https://ssrn.com/abstract=2015616.

Riches, Lousia. "The United Nations Human Rights Council: A Critique and Early Assessment," Asian Journal of International Law, Vol. 5, Issue 2 (July 2015), pp. 415–416.

Salamatin, M. (2020) 'China's Belt and Road Initiative is Reshaping Human Rights Norms', Vanderbilt Journal of Transnational Law, 53(4), pp. 1427–1476.

Seddigh, M. and Mosavi, S. A. (2015) 'UN Responsibility towards Actions against International Regulations (Comprehensive Study of UN Human Rights Council on Gaza War)', International Studies Journal (ISJ), 12(4), pp. 129–146.

Sharvit Baruch, Pnina, The Report of the Human Rights Council Commission of Inquiry on the 2014 Operation in the Gaza Strip – A Critical Analysis (December 7, 2016). Israel Yearbook on Human Rights VOL 46 p. 29, Available at SSRN: https://ssrn.com/abstract=2881897.

Shelton, Dinah L., Standard-Setting by the United Nations Commission on Human Rights: An Overview from Its Inception in 1947 until the Creation of the Human

Rights Council in 2006 (2008). 29 Human Rights Law Journal 15 (2008), GWU Legal Studies Research Paper No. 2013-27, GWU Law School Public Law Research Paper No. 2013-27, Available at SSRN: https://ssrn.com/abstract=2225912.

Sinagra, Augusto, The United Nations Human Rights Council and the Right to Peace (October 1, 2016). Cross-Border Journal for International Studies no.1/2016, Available at SSRN: https://ssrn.com/abstract=2993182.

Smith, R. K. M. (2011) 'More of the Same or Something Different? Preliminary Observations on the Contribution of Universal Periodic Review with Reference to the Chinese Experience', Chinese Journal of International Law, 10(3), pp. 565–586.

Subedi, Surya P. and Wheatley, Steven M. and Mukherjee, Amrita and Ngane, Sylvia Ntube, The Role of the Special Rapporteurs of the United Nations Human Rights Council in the Development and Promotion of International Human Rights Norms (2011). The International Journal of Human Rights, Vol. 15, No. 2, pp. 155–161, 2011, Available at SSRN: https://ssrn.com/abstract=1895671.

Thiele, B. and Gomez, M. (2011) 'United Nations Human Rights Council', Netherlands Quarterly of Human Rights, 29(2), pp. 212–219.

Tistounet, Eric The UN Human Rights Council. A Practical Anatomy. (Elgar Practical Guides). London, Elgar Publishers, 2020.

Tomuschat Christian, Human Rights. Between Idealism and Realism. Third Edition. Oxford, University Press, 2014.

United Nations, Commissions of Inquiry and Fact-Finding Missions on International Human Rights and Humanitarian Law. Guidance and Practice. United Nations Office of the High Commissioner for Human Rights, New York and Geneva, 2015.

Vengoechea-Barrios, J. (2008) 'The Universal Periodic Review: A New Hope for International Human Rights Law or a Reformulation of Errors of the Past?', International Law, (13), pp. 101–116.

Viegas e Silva, Marisa, The United Nations Human Rights Council: Six Years On (March 1, 2013). SUR International Journal on Human Rights, v. 10, n. 18, Jun. 2013, Available at SSRN: https://ssrn.com/abstract=2399611 or http://dx.doi.org/10.2139/ssrn.2399611.

Voss, M. J. (2019) 'The Use (or Misuse) of Amendments to Contest Human Rights Norms at the UN Human Rights Council', Human Rights Review, 20(4), p. 397.

Voss, M. J. (2019) 'The Use (or Misuse) of Amendments to Contest Human Rights Norms at the UN Human Rights Council', Human Rights Review, 20(4), pp. 397–422.

Voss, M. J. (no date) 'Contesting human rights and climate change at the UN human rights council', Journal of Human Rights and the Environment, 11(1), pp. 6–29. doi: 10.4337/jhre.2020.01.01.

Wewerinke-Singh, Margaretha, Climate Change, Human Rights and the International Legal Order: The Role of the UN Human Rights Council (October 1, 2013). Available at SSRN: https://ssrn.com/abstract=2908992 or http://dx.doi.org/10.2139/ssrn.2908992.

Zalnieriute, Monika, The Necessity for Binding Human Rights Obligations for Private Actors in the Digital Age: A Submission to the UN Human Rights Council on New and Emerging Technologies (October 15, 2019). UNSW Law Research Paper No. 19-81, Available at SSRN: https://ssrn.com/abstract=3470951 or http://dx.doi.org/10.2139/ssrn.3470951.

Zhu, Lijiang "International Humanitarian Law in the Universal Periodic Review of the U.N. Human Rights Council An Empirical Survey," Journal of International Humanitarian legal Studies 5 (2014) 186–212. | D O I 1 0 .1 1 6 3.

Index

www.ingramcontent.com/pod-product-compliance
Lightning Source LLC
Chambersburg PA
CBHW031324230926
51848CB00001B/85
9789004504943